WEEK IN— WEEK OUT

A New Look at Liturgical Preaching

DAVID E. BABIN

A Crossroad Book

THE SEABURY PRESS • NEW YORK

The Seabury Press
815 Second Avenue
New York, N.Y. 10017

Copyright © 1976 by The Seabury Press, Inc.
Printed in the United States of America

LIBRARY OF CONGRESS CATALOGING IN PUBLICATION DATA

Babin, David E
Week in week out.

Includes bibliographical references.
1.   Preaching.   I.   Title.
BV4211.2.B224 C.2 251   75-37814
ISBN 0-8164-0287-6

*To Bob Rodenmayer
who started it all.*

CONTENTS

Preface   ix

PART ONE
THE CONTEXT OF PREACHING,   1

Chapter 1   Week in—week out   3
         2   Communicating the Word   11
         3   The *Word* in Words   18
         4   The Preacher as Medium as Message   27
         5   The Sermon as Monolog/Dialog   41
         6   Liturgical Preaching: 1   52
         7   Liturgical Preaching: 2   61

PART TWO
GETTING IT ALL TOGETHER,   69

Chapter 8   "Gospelling"   71
         9   The Celebration of Health   79
        10   Chapter and Verse   87
        11   Making Your Point   98
        12   A Specialized Form of Liturgical Preaching 114
        13   On Having the Last Word   118

             Notes   128

PREFACE

The proclamation of the Gospel is essential to the mission of the Church. This book is predicated on the truth of that proposition, coupled with the equally firmly held conviction that that mission can be furthered significantly by effective liturgical preaching. I believe that much of what is wrong with preaching today is that many of us do not have a clear idea of just what it is and what might realistically be expected of it. What is called for is not "more of the same, only better," but a whole new concept of preaching.

The first part of the book is an effort to rethink the very nature of liturgical preaching, its role and function, and even its definition. The second part is devoted to translating theory into practical suggestions for the actual process of preparing and presenting the liturgical sermon.

Throughout, I have tried to take seriously the insights of recent theology, psychology, and communication theory and to apply these directly and specifically to the proclamation of the Good News week in, week out. This demands a frank appraisal of the limitations as well as the possibilities of liturgical preaching and involves what may be a radical redefinition of biblical preaching.

The second half of the book includes a detailed step-by-step method of preparing the liturgical sermon. A relatively new and specialized form of liturgical preaching is examined, and the final chapter contains some concrete suggestions for the establishment, care, and feeding of sermon preparation and feedback groups.

At times I may have been ruthless in my criticism of prevailing concepts and practices of preaching in order to arrive at more realistic definitions and expectations. Overall, it has been my intention to support those men and women whose joyful work it is to share the living Word with fellow members of the Body of Christ week in, week out.

Portions of Part One have previously appeared in different form as articles by the author in *Anglican Theological Review* and *Preaching,* and I am grateful for permission to use this material.

A special acknowledgment of appreciation is made to the following practicing preachers on the island of Oahu—clergy members of the Windward Coalition of Churches, Kailua, or the Episcopal Diocese of Hawaii—who so graciously served as a test group for this work, reading all or parts of the manuscript and offering many helpful criticisms and suggestions: Bil Aulenbach, Jack Belton, Mike Carlson, Claude Du Teil, Lee Gable, Eugene Harshman, Ken Heflin, Alan Mark, Joe Pummil, E. W. Reynolds, Roy Sasaki, Warren Studer, Masayoshi Wakai, and John Wetzel. Gentlemen, for your *kokua, mahalo.*

DAVID E. BABIN

Kailua beaches
August, 1975.

WEEK IN—WEEK OUT

PART ONE

The Context of Preaching

As Others See Us

There is, perhaps, no greater hardship at present inflicted on mankind in civilised and free countries, than the necessity of listening to sermons. No one but a preaching clergyman has, in these realms, the power of compelling an audience to sit silent and be tormented. No one but a preaching clergyman can revel in platitudes, truisms, and untruisms, and yet receive, as his undisputed privilege, the same respectful demeanour as though words of impassioned eloquence, or persuasive logic, fell from his lips. Let a professor of law or physic find his place in a lecture-room, and there pour forth jejune words and useless empty phrases, and he will pour them forth to empty benches. Let a barrister attempt to talk without talking well, and he will talk but seldom. A judge's charge need be listened to per force by none but the jury, prisoner, and gaoler. A member of Parliament can be coughed down or counted out. Town councilors can be tabooed. But no one can rid himself of the preaching clergyman. He is the bore of the age, the old man whom we Sindbads cannot shake off, the nightmare that disturbs our Sunday's rest, the incubus that overloads our religion and makes God's service distasteful. We are not forced into church! No: but we desire more than that. We desire not to be forced to stay away. We desire, nay, we are resolute, to enjoy the comfort of public worship; but we desire also that we may do so without an amount of tedium which ordinary human nature cannot endure with patience; that we may be able to leave the house of God without that anxious longing to escape, which is the common consequence of common sermons.

Anthony Trollope, *Barchester Towers.*

But take heart. Robert Louis Stevenson in *Travels With A Donkey* remarks at one point in his diary: "Sunday. Went to church this morning, but was not too bored."

Chapter
1
WEEK IN—WEEK OUT

EARLIER this week an estimated seventy-five million Americans gathered themselves in over three hundred thousand different groups across the land. In virtually every community in the United States, from tiny hamlets to major metropolitan centers, they assembled in groups of from four to several thousand people—forming in the aggregate the largest single human resource available in the nation.

In case you missed it last week, you'll be given another opportunity to participate in this vast colligation, for it will be repeated again next Sunday morning and the Sunday following that, and the next Sunday and the next, into the unforeseeable future—just as it has been every Sunday morning in this country since the sixteenth century, and in Europe and the Mediterranean countries for fifteen hundred years before that. Over a hundred thousand Sundays—week in, week out.

The number of Christians throughout the whole world who participate in the worship of God on any given Sunday make up a figure too staggering for the mind to deal with; trying to imagine seventy-five million Americans is mind-stretching enough. And incredibly, all those people gather into those hundreds of thousands of congregations for essentially the same purpose: the worship of God: Father, Son, and Holy Spirit. The various congregations will effect that worship by a wide variety of rites and ceremonies, a few of which will be distasteful, if not downright repugnant to some. But the majority will be remarkably similar in broad outline while displaying an incredible diversity in style and detail.

Whatever their differences might be, virtually every one of the more than three hundred thousand congregations will share at least one element of ceremony. Practically every one of those seventy-five million Christians will go to church next Sunday—or any Sunday—expecting to hear the Word of God proclaimed and expounded in some sort of sermon. Whether it is called a sermon, a homily, a witness, a message, or a word, the expectation will be filled by nearly a third of a million preachers, some ordained, some not.

The strange, even tragic, fact is that very few of those millions of churchgoers, and fewer still of the hundreds of thousands of preachers, will have any expectation whatsoever that anything will actually *happen* as a result of all that preaching, that anything will be changed much by it. And that expectation, too (or the lack of it)), most surely will be fulfilled. This is probably the chief reason why another sixty million or so Christians are not among those who gather on any given Sunday. Most of them don't feel they have missed much. A few might inquire of a friend, "What did the preacher say?" Probably none will ask, "What *happened* at church on Sunday?"

If the idea of over three hundred thousand sermons saturating the air on any given Sunday morning fills you with some apprehension (as it does me), concentrate on your own parish church for just a minute. Let's say there are two hundred and fifty people in your parish church next Sunday morning (the national average). If they are exposed to twenty minutes of preaching, that represents over eighty man-hours invested in that single sermon. Add to that the preacher's own preparation time of five to ten hours. Already, in one parish, we have quite a considerable investment of time.

But there is even more to take into account. Most churches, that is, the worship centers themselves, are in use only during the hours of formal worship. For a majority of parishes this means only for a few hours on Sunday mornings. The expenditure of time, money, thought, and energy that are brought to bear upon that hour or two is enormous. Consider the time of the musicians, the cost of the music and organ, the hours of practice and planning; the work of the sexton, altar guild, ushers, lay readers, and acolytes; the prorated cost of the building, its maintenance, heat, lights, cost of furniture, books, decorations, and appurtenances—all this and more is focused upon and concentrated in one or two brief hours on Sunday morning. And probably thirty to forty percent of that time is devoted to the sermon.

Dare we multiply all those hours, all that energy and thought and care, all that financial value, by three hundred thousand congregations in the United States? Or by the vastly larger number throughout the world? And then extend that to the number of Sundays in the Christian era—both past and future? No, even the implications for a single parish for a single year are enough to tax one's comprehension. My little desk calculator blew a fuse while I was just trying to compile the bare statistics. But surely so vast a human and material resource was never assembled for any other single enterprise.

In spite of holding minimal expectations for the consequences of the sermon, many churchgoers express liking for and appreciation of preaching. However, the existence of the sermon as an integral part of the worship experience of most Christians is not primarily a matter of taste or choice; it is, generally speaking, a given. Preaching is not merely provided for in most liturgical formularies, it is actually required by the rites used by an overwhelming majority of congregations.

The sermon, in fact, is probably the single most widely accepted, most common weekly liturgical practice among Christians throughout the world. The remarkably diverse denominations, sects, groups, and subgroups that call themselves Christian may disagree (sometimes violently) about the place or even the existence of sacraments, the use of music, or the role of clergy in worship, but virtually all acknowledge that preaching is, and should be, an integral part of the Sunday worship experience. For some the sermon virtually *is* the liturgy, for others it is an indispensible element, and for many it is the keystone of their worship. Like the liturgy itself, preaching has been a normal part of the regular worship of Christians for nearly two thousand years.

Without a broad, solid base of support, nothing could gain and hold such a favored, universally accepted position in the weekly worship of groups who have almost no other liturgical practice in common. In the case of preaching, this support comes from several quarters, all of which converge to form an apparently unshakeable foundation.

First of all, there is the example of our Lord himself preaching in the synagogue at Capernaum. But, of course, this was pre-Christian worship. The famous sermons of Peter on the day of Pentecost and of Stephen before the council may have carried some cumulative weight in establishing the importance of preaching; but neither of these occasions was in a liturgical context, so they probably would not be considered normative for regular worship. Far more influential would be the practice of Paul, who apparently preached whenever and wherever Christians gathered to worship. (And Paul was a marathon preacher—no twenty-minute limit for him!) Numerous references in the later epistles and other books of the New Testament give ample indication that from the very beginning the sermon was a normal and expected element in the worship experience of the young Church.

If the role of preaching in the context of the liturgy was well established by biblical precedent and apostolic practice, it was amply reinforced by the early Fathers of the Church and conscientiously maintained as the Church grew and expanded. Clement, Ignatius, Origen, Cyprian, Paul of Samosta, and of course the great "Golden Tongue," Chrysostom—all are names familiar to any student of early Church history, and all of them practiced, promoted, and furthered the art of preaching. Indeed, some of the earliest Church Fathers are known to us chiefly because of their preaching or through their sermons themselves.

In subsequent centuries Church leaders felt so strongly about the continuing need for regular, sound preaching that they caused to be published a continuous stream of books containing instructions on the preparation and delivery of sermons, exegetical and homiletical aids, and even complete homilies for those clergy whose education or inspiration was not up to the demanding task of regular preparation or the maintenance of the high standards hoped for by the ecclesiastical authorities. It certainly is true that, as was the case with other liturgical practices, the fortunes of preaching waxed and waned at various times during the history of the Church. At certain times, in certain places, preaching would be allowed to deteriorate drastically, even to the point of becoming a liturgical oddity inserted into the worship only on special occasions. At other times, and meanwhile in other parts of the Church, preaching would be done enthusiastically and skillfully.

In the sixteenth century apparently many of the Reformation leaders would have preferred to retain the practice of weekly Eucharist, but since most were adamant about abolishing celebrations of the Lord's Supper where the congregation was not prepared to communicate, they had little success in restoring the practice of weekly Communion among their followers. Thus, they were faced with the necessity of formulating worship services without the Mass, which had been the foundation of the Sunday liturgical experience since the earliest days of the Church. Naturally, they responded with a wide variety of liturgical innovations. The one element that was retained by virtually all the reformers was preaching. In fact, many of the protesting congregations began to use the sermon as the key element of their Sunday worship and to build whatever liturgical expressions they felt appropriate around that central act.

No one seemed to bother too much about the actual theological rationale for preaching until more recent times. From time to time it had been passionately espoused as a good and important thing to do, but most of the argument was based upon historical precedence and pastoral concern rather than theological constructs. Recently, however, the theology of preaching has been thoroughly explored and well established by a plethora of distinguished scholars representing almost every principal stream of Christian thought. Protestant, Roman Catholic, and Orthodox theologians have systematically and dogmatically presented the theological case for preaching. In general, the Protestants are anxious to show that preaching is a legitimate enterprise to be placed alongside, but not to replace, the sacramental ministry of the Church. Roman Catholics, on the other hand, are equally determined to demonstrate the sacramental nature of preaching itself and to restore it to respectability in the Catholic tradition.

Happily, they both end up saying pretty much the same thing, and together they present a formidable, and almost unquestionable theological foundation for the principle of preaching as an effective means of transmitting the grace of God (whatever the various writers may mean by that). Theologically, preaching plays a role that is not merely an adjunct to the liturgical and pastoral ministry of the Church, but is a necessity to the full, ongoing mission of the body of Christ. Herbert H. Farmer once made the striking observation that other religions might lose all their books and followers and yet "substantially the same religion reappear. . . . But were all Christian records and all Christians extirpated, Christianity could not recur again. In its recurrence without a preacher, without a witness, it would flatly contradict all that it had always claimed to be. To put it paradoxically, in happening again it would show that it had never, according to its own definition of itself, happened at all." In other words, Christianity is a preached religion, not an intellectual or ethical system. While it is both reasonable and rational, it never could be deduced logically because one of the essential elements is a witness to bring in the Good News.

Likewise, the theologians have established virtually unassailable grounds for the sacramental nature of preaching. The Orthodox scholar Alexander Schmemann can go so far as to say that it "transforms the human words of the Gospel into the Word of God and the manifestation of the kingdom. And it transforms the man who hears the Word into a receptacle of the Word and a temple of the Spirit. [Therefore,] *the proclamation of the word is a sacramental act par excellence.*" And Edward H. Schillebeeckx comes to the conclusion that "at its peak, the word itself becomes sacrament."

Any one of these three factors—the scriptural precedence, the unbroken tradition of nearly two thousand years, or the theological arguments of scholars of many different persuasions —might have been sufficient to ensure the role of the sermon as an integral part of regular Christian worship. Taken together they constitute such a formidable case that the sermon would seem destined to maintain its honored position on Sunday morning.

Yet, in the face of all this, the validity of the preaching enterprise is being challenged from many quarters. It seems to me that enough of this challenge is coming from responsible churchmen and is of such gravity that it deserves to be taken seriously. On the one hand, the very strength of the role of the sermon is being used as the basis for raising some disturbing questions. Acknowledging the incredible resources involved—in human time and energy as well as financial and material investment— is the sermon the best use we can make of these considerable resources? Is it good stewardship to continue to commit this vast wealth to the preaching enterprise? Can we be doing something —anything—to spread the Gospel and promote the mission of the

Church that would show a greater return on the investment than the sermon?

At the same time, another serious challenge is issuing from the fact of our technological age and from world views and life-styles drastically different from those of any previous period of the Church's history. Is the sermon still a viable means of communicating the Gospel in the age of electronic media? Is it still possible for the Word of God to be mediated through the words of a sermon? The radical questions are: Can the sermon be an effective means of communication today? Is it a medium through which the Word of God can still be heard?

My own answer to this set of questions is an enthusiastic "Yes," followed by a qualified "but . . ." And what follows the "but" is crucial to the continued viability and effectiveness of preaching. Existence is not justified merely by the fact of its being there. Furthermore, the very fact of the prominent place of preaching in the whole fabric of the Church's worship and the heavy investment we all have both in worship in general and in preaching in particular obliges us to listen carefully to some fundamental questions about role, place, and effectiveness of the sermon. We can no longer continue to take it for granted that preaching *should* be a part of our regular worship experience. Rather, we must begin to take a searching look at what realistically might be expected from preaching, and to explore some of the ways that expectation might be realized. Our investigation must begin with a concept of communication, for whatever else the proclamation of the Word of God might entail, it surely has something to do with communication; and the sermon is at least one form of communication.

Chapter
2
COMMUNICATING THE WORD

WHEN *Webster's Third New International Dictionary—Unabridged* was published in 1961, the editor-in-chief wrote a lengthy introduction to the volume which included this remarkable statement: "It is now fairly clear that before the twentieth century is over every community in the world will have learned how to communicate with all the rest of humanity."

That certainly will be a glorious day! I must confess to being not nearly so optimistic as the editor-in-chief of *Webster's*. In fact, what seems to me to be "now fairly clear" is that people who already use the same dictionary, even members of the same household, find communication difficult at best and, at times, impossible. And yet it has been amply demonstrated by anthropology, psychology, sociology, theology, and a host of other disciplines, that the human being begins to realize his potentiality only in a social context—that is, only in relation to other human beings, and communication is the agent by which this relationship is established and maintained. Communication is the key to the development, and even to the awareness, of one's own personhood. Denied access to any communication with other human beings, one becomes something less than human.

It has also been shown that the more alike creatures are, the

11

fuller their communication can be. It certainly is possible for various animals to transmit messages to members of other species, but nothing like full communication can take place except between members of the same species. Of all known creatures, the potential for full community is highest among human beings; therefore, the fullest degree of communication is to be realized among humans. This is an important part of the significance of the symbol "made in the image of God." God created us with the potential for the fullest kind of communication with him. Without that stamp, anything approaching full communication would have been impossible. With it, made in God's own image, man can know God and be known of him. It seems to me that a primary goal of preaching is to transmit the message that we *can* be in communication with God, to enable that communion, and to *engage in it*.

What would that kind of communication mean? What would it look like? The word itself gives us some clues:

Com-MUN-ication
Com-MUN-icate
Com-MUN-icant
Com-MUN-ion
Com-MUN-ity
Com-MUN-ist
Com-MUN-al
Com-MUN-e
Com-MON

What all these words have in common is the word "common," which is derived from the Latin root *munia* plus the prefix *com*. *Munia* means services or aid or assistance. When the prefix is added, it means mutual service or aid. Additional prefixes were sometimes added. For instance, one who had been a part of the mutual interaction but for some reason was no longer allowed to be, was *ex-commun*. One who, by reason of age or infirmity or perhaps high office, was no longer expected to contribute to the mutual interaction but was allowed to benefit from it, was *immune*.

Communicate is, of course, the verb form of communication. It is interesting to note that in Church language to communicate means to receive the body and blood of Christ at the Eucharist. And to communicate means to engage in communication. A communicant is one who communicates. A Church communicant is one who participates in the Holy Eucharist, frequently called Holy Communion. In other words, the whole eucharistic act is closely related to the concept of communication. A community is made up of communicants, persons who communicate. A communist, speaking not politically but etymologically, would be one who espouses or engages in communion . . . among communicants . . . who communicate . . . in a community. And so on down the list. [What does it mean to speak of Christian traditions that are—or that are not—in communion with one another? How does a phrase such as "The Anglican communion" differ from "The Anglican community?"]

By now, we are beginning to see some of the richness of meaning available to those who seek to define and speak of communication. The dictionary makes a helpful distinction between communicate and impart. Impart, it explains, stresses sharing with another or with others that which primarily is one's own. Communicate, on the other hand, stresses making *common* to all that which formerly had belonged only to one or to a few.

Common usage reveals at least three different definitions of communication. According to the first of these, communication occurs whenever something—anything—is perceived by a human receiver, whether or not that "thing" is consciously intended by the sender. Under this definition, some sort of communication takes place whenever any two people meet. In fact, they need not actually meet; one might have sent the other a letter, for instance. Several years ago a librarian in our seminary became a father and wished to inform a friend of this startling event. The friend happened to be living in England at the time, so the proud father sent a cablegram reading: STEVEN DOUGLAS CALDWELL SEVEN POUNDS TWO OUNCES. When the cablegram was telephoned to the friend's residence, the message was taken by a slightly deaf housekeeper. The friend arrived home to discover a note reading: THE VENT DOESN'T DRAW WELL. HEAVEN SOUNDS TOO FANCY. In spite of the garbled message, one could say that a communication had been sent and a communication had been received.

It should be noted that communication, in this and any of the definitions to follow, need not be verbal. We frequently send and receive some of our most important communications nonverbally. Sometimes we give or receive what we call "mixed signals." This might occur when the words say, or seem to say, one thing while the nonverbal (perhaps through the medium of body language) seems to be saying something entirely different or even opposite. Probably the sender *intends* only one of these messages to come across. However, the receiver can say that the sender communicated something quite different than that which he intended. The emphasis of this definition is upon the event. That event—communication—either does or does not occur. It cannot be said to fail, and questions of relative value cannot be applied to the communication itself although they may, of course, be applied to the effect.

A second definition says that communication occurs when the message received is more or less similar to that intended by the sender. This is the definition usually used by mass media and public media people. It is also the definition most frequently intended by public speakers and entertainers and sometimes by preachers. Here the emphasis is upon content, and obviously the communication *can* fail, wholly or in part.

The third definition involves a response from the receiver. In this instance communication is said to occur when the receiver responds in such a way as to indicate that the message was received, the degree to which he understood or believed that he understood, and usually some indication of the effect of the message. Now we have two messages: from A to B and from B to A. Communication is seen as a two-way, ongoing process. Logically, A would then have to respond to B, then B to A, and so on indefinitely. In practice, of course, the process is interrupted somewhere short of the infinite. This definition emphasizes process, but it also implies an effect. Like the previous definition, it can fail altogether or be judged partially successful.

These several definitions of communication frequently are diagrammed by straight-line models which in their simplest forms look like this:

Definitions 1 & 2   *Definition 3*

The third definition also lends itself to a more sophisticated helical model:

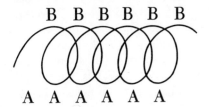

This diagram makes it clear that having initiated the process, A is then influenced by it and is not in quite the same position he was in previously. The same is true with B. With each transaction, both A and B change somewhat.

Both the definitions and the diagrams given above are reduced to their simplest forms. Actually, no self-respecting communications theorist would stop there—most wouldn't even begin there. The definitions can take pages of textual explanation and the diagrams can become so sophisticated that they require newsprint-size paper, plastic overlays, different colors for different aspects of the transaction, and so forth. But what they all come down to is either a straight line from A to B, and perhaps back again, or a curving line that never ends up quite where it began, resulting in a helix.

Some theorists have begun to use another definition which requires an entirely different kind of diagram: an ellipse with two or more foci:

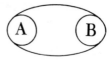

In this diagram, the communication is that which lies inside the ellipse, and it incorporates the foci. The communication is not identical with either A or B, nor is it a combination or amalgamation of the two. It is a new thing, partly shaped by the communicants and dependent upon them, but also partly with its own shape not determined by the subjects. (The persons involved are both subjects and objects.) Furthermore, the communication is something for which the several communicants are mutually responsible—something they have formed and hold in common. In one sense, then, communication does not create community, it presupposes it. On the other hand, communication gives shape and substance and meaning to community.

Furthermore, communication is seen to be an experience in process. It is in the dynamic of the interaction between the persons involved. Communication is always potentiality; it is never closed, in the sense of *finis*. One would think that communication is a common enough experience that, although not everyone might be able to define it exactly, almost anyone would recognize when it occurs. However, I believe it to be vital to the preaching enterprise that preachers know as precisely as possible both the possibilities and the limitations of the sermon. If preaching is intended to be a form of communication, then identification of those potentials and limits depends upon the definition chosen, for each possible definition has certain implications peculiar to itself.

The final definition given above seems to me the most useful, especially as regards preaching. Therefore, this will be the meaning intended by the word "communication" as it is used throughout this book. The implications of this choice will become clear as we proceed, but the first and most obvious of these is: given this definition, it becomes illogical, even impossible, to say, "I have something I wish to communicate *to* the people of my congregation." Rather, we are urged to say, "I have something to communicate *with* them." This may include the transmission of certain information as well as the expression of my own attitudes about that information, but if that is all that is intended, then the transaction stops short of communication.

Which brings us to one of the principal ways human beings have of effecting communication: the use of words.

Chapter

3

THE WORD IN WORDS

IT IS said that Abraham Lincoln once asked his son Tad how many legs his dog had. Unhesitatingly, the boy replied, "Four." Then Lincoln said, "Suppose we call that appendage that protrudes from the dog's rear end a leg. Now, how many legs does the dog have?" To which Tad naturally answered, "Five." But Lincoln disagreed: "No matter what you and I may call that thing that wags from the back end of the dog's body, it's still a tail, and the dog still really has only four legs."

There is a lot of folk wisdom in that little tale (pun intended). If everyone else calls that fifth appendage a tail, it *is* a tail no matter what word the Lincolns might use to refer to it. Used only between themselves, the misnomer probably would not cause any confusion. But for the Lincolns to forget or ignore the fact that the rest of the world used the word leg to refer only to the four limbs that support the dog's body would be a serious impediment to effective communication about the dog with anyone else. Conversely, if everyone else used the word leg to refer to all five appendages, even though one of them differed markedly from the others, the dog would have five legs.

The point is that it does matter what we call a thing—how we name it. My grandfather, a doctor, once had a patient who functioned quite well vis-à-vis the things of the world and who had a very high intelligence, but a tumor on his brain caused him to misname familiar objects. For instance, he could readily identify a watch, he knew its purpose and even exactly how it worked. Ask him what that thing was and he would reply that it was a shoe. What do you do with a shoe? Why, you tell time with it, of course. And it was this way with all objects. Imagine the disability of a man whose thought processes in every other respect exceeded the average, yet who could not order a meal in a restaurant.

Each thing in the world is not just any thing; it is a particular thing, and it has a name. This name may, and usually does, vary from one language to another, even from one culture to another although both may use the same written language. But within a community of people who speak the same language, using a common vocabulary, each thing known to them has a commonly agreed upon name. Some objects have more than one name, depending upon the precision of description, but in such cases the various names are commonly agreed upon.

The possession of a spoken language is a powerful tool, and the prerogative to name the objects of creation has been cherished by the human race since ancient times. To know the name of a thing or of a person is to wield a certain power over the one whose name is known. We learn the importance and power of naming quite early. Preschool children will chant: "Sticks and stones may break my bones, but words will never hurt me." Actually, the chant is a defensive measure and a lie, for the child knows, as we all do, that no physical injuries can cause the pain of certain words, especially when those words are spoken by someone who matters to us. Likewise, there is no greater pleasure than that experienced upon the hearing of certain words from the lips of someone we love. Among adults, name-calling may be disparaged as a shabby political tactic, but still it is one of the most successful methods of depriving one's opponent of votes (although not necessarily winning them for oneself).

The ancient documents of the Book of Genesis time and again stress the power of name-calling and name-knowing. The prerogative to name creatures is given to man by God himself, thereby giving to man some of the divine power. Jacob would not release the angel until he knew his name; such knowledge would give the wrestler the final victory in spite of his physcial injuries. God was loath to reveal his own name even to his most devoted servants. Later, use of the name of God was so tightly restricted that the actual pronunciation has been lost if it was ever really known. And when God wished to thwart the goal of mankind to become as gods, he employed the effective tactic of destroying the larger community by confusing their language, making it impossible for the various smaller communities of people to communicate with one another. The sign of the creation of the new community through the gift of the Holy Spirit was the breaking down of language barriers and the restoration of communication. Theologically, all this comes to fruition in the Fourth Gospel where the Word of God *is* the Son of God.

Sooner or later, most theological investigation into the nature of preaching falls back upon an examination of the Word of God as a biblical concept. The approach is sound, and a thorough exploration of that avenue reveals some features frequently overlooked by many theologians and given less attention than they deserve by others. "Word of God" is an Old Testament expression for the act of God addressing himself to man. E. H. Schillebeeckx has done an admirable job of summarizing this concept in an article that appeared in the Winter 1969 issue of *Listening,* and the following paragraphs are indebted to his work.

In reading the Old Testament, we discover that the Hebrew term customarily translated as "word" is the same expression used to denote an event or an act. Furthermore, the word acts, as though the word itself were an effective agent. The words of a man are the very life of the man—the person himself. Hebrew does not distinguish between the person who speaks and his words.

What is true for human beings is likewise true for God; or rather, it is true for humans *because* it is first of all true for God. Thus, the Word of God creates an historical fact. When this Word of God is spoken through men and women, it is called prophecy because it creates history on the one hand and explains it on the other; it brings about the future and interprets the events. Because it is the Word of God, it is truth, while the words of false gods are lies and are without efficacy. The words of the prophet carry the force of the Word of God because the prophet is a "man of God."

Moreover, the Word of God is the incarnation of the will of God in history and in nature. "We live by everything that comes from the mouth of God" means that we live by the Word of God. The Word of God, then, is both revelation and response. God's Word comes to man through man or through an earthly event, but the people become fully aware of it through the interpretation and response-word of the prophet. The Word, then, *is* the saving act of God, apprehended by his people as the "men of God" listen to, respond to, and interpret it to the people. When God reveals himself in Christ, the Word becomes manifest in human form. Now, the Word of God speaks directly to his people through human words.

As a mode of revelation, this biblical concept finds corroboration in modern philosophy as well as in the field of communication theory. Such diverse thinkers as Martin Heidegger, Maurice Merleau-Ponty, and L. S. Vigotsky, all assert that it is in speaking that man realizes life. The point is succinctly put by Georges Gusdorf in *Speaking* (1965): "To come into the world is to begin making a speech." He goes on to say that speaking is the beginning of existence. Obviously Gusdorf is not talking about the biological process but about humanity, personality. Phenomenologists, linguistic philosophers, learning theorists, all agree that we create our world by the way we learn to speak.

Notice that we *learn* to speak; we learn our language from others. Language is a much broader category than vocabulary, syntax, and grammar; it includes the interpretation of the total environment or whatever portion of that environment is sensorally perceived. Still, most (some would say all) of the nonverbal is identified with or actually translated into words because verbal language is our primary tool for thought. Both what we think and how we think are determined in large measure by the way we have learned to use language.

We may learn the definitions of words from the dictionary, but dictionary definitions are lifeless. They are valuable to us only when they resonate with some experience. We learn the meaning of words (as opposed to the definition) by hearing them used in situations where life is being lived. That is why many Christians might be able to give a quite acceptable definition of, let us say, the word "redemption" without having any idea of its real meaning. It is not that they do not *know* the meaning of the word, it is rather that the word actually has no meaning for them. This may be because the person has never had the experience that we would call redemptive, or simply because no one ever identified that experience for him. If the definition can be given in such a way as to resonate with his experience, and he hears it named, he might have what teachers sometimes call an "Ah-ha!" experience. Remember the story of the schoolboy who was delighted to learn that he had been writing prose for years?

We have noted previously that words are not the only means of communication; they do not make up the totality of our language. Even so, after all this is acknowledged and even emphasized, it still remains that we are word-thinking, word-using creatures. Our own self-understanding is largely, perhaps entirely, shaped by our vocabulary. And so words are our primary tools of interpersonal communication. Preaching, too, is more than words, and the nonverbal factors weigh more heavily than most preachers or listeners realize. Still, words are an indispensable element of the sermon. In fact, the sermon is one way of organizing the Word into words, of articulating and identifying an experience. It is a way of bringing into being—that is, bringing to bear in a particular place at a particular time with particular people—the saving act of God.

Having said this, let me now make clear that a sermon is not a *medium* of communication, at least not in a primary or base sense. It is, rather, an instrument or a tool or a technique employed by the actual primary medium: the preacher. This distinction is made to point up the fact that the message, the content, does not originate with the preacher; it originates with God. The preacher is a medium employed by God to effect the communication between God and his people.

There are a number of methods for organizing the Word into words—all of which at one time or another might be, and usually are, utilized by one who intends to witness to the Good News. The most obvious of these is writing. But writing is primarily a method of transmitting information and revealing the author's attitudes. Seldom, if ever, does one experience the dynamic of communication through the written word. This is not intended to denigrate the usefulness or importance of writing (after all, I am devoting the major portion of a sabbatical leave to writing). It is simply to point out the essential difference between the written and the spoken word. This can best be illustrated by the way we usually experience the sermon. Obviously one of the drawbacks to any oral presentation is that some words might be inaudible, and the listener cannot use what he cannot hear; another is that the listener's attention might wander for a greater or lesser period of time, and he can never regain that which has been spoken during that interlude; and yet another is that the listener doesn't have a text to refer back to as the sermon progresses.

All these problems could be solved by having the sermon written out, duplicated, and distributed to members of the congregation as they arrive or at some appropriate point in the service. Then, when the time came for the sermon, the preacher might just announce that the organist would play a little soft background music for twenty or thirty minutes while

everyone read the sermon at their own speed. After all, most of
our congregations are literate. Special arrangements would have
to be made for the blind, of course. For those who read rapidly,
there could be some discussion-type questions at the end to
think about while the others went on reading. The very slow
readers could simply take the text home with them and finish it
at their leisure.

Why does this suggestion sound ridiculous? Because we need
and desire more than information. What we really long for, and
desperately hope for, is some real personal engagement, for
communication, for the kind of sharing that both shapes us and
is shaped by us. No matter how skillful the author may be, this
kind of personal engagement is seldom effected through the
written word.

The lecture is a valuable technique for organizing words
orally. Yet one might lecture on a subject quite lucidly without
having any sort of personal commitment to it. One might easily
teach about a subject without even believing it, certainly
without having any personal experience of it. For instance, a
few years ago, at the request of several students, I taught a class
on atheism. I am not an atheist, have never been one, and do
not believe in the point of view espoused by atheists. In the
process of the course, I learned quite a bit about the subject;
but I could never have witnessed to an experience as an atheist.
In fact, that class really got off the ground only when we
brought in an atheist who tried to convert us all. I'm pleased to
say that he did not succeed, but what he did as a bona fide
witness was something far different than I could do as a teacher.

Teaching is important; but it is not the same thing as preaching. The purpose of the sermon is not primarily pedagogical.
One who has had an experience does not try to argue the relative merits of his system of thought or analyze data; he de-
scribes that experience, the authority it has for him, and the
implications of it for his life. One of the most humorous and
touching stories in the Fourth Gospel is the account of the man

who was born blind and healed by Jesus. Before the learned
doctors of the Jewish council he was unable to account intellec-
tually for what had happened to him, but the fact of that experience, and its meaning for him, could not be denied.

Obviously, communication can and does take place in the
teaching situation. What I am saying is that teaching has its own
set of goals, expectations, and techniques and that these are not
the same as those for preaching.

A third and very effective instrument is the one-to-one personal conversation. Here, the potential for full communication
seems to be the highest of all. It is, or can be, oral. Furthermore, the speech can be tailored directly to an individual person and a particular situation. Corrections in language can be
made as they occur and semantic misunderstandings clarified.
Also, on this level other nonverbal tools can be taken into account and utilized. Unfortunately, the Sunday morning liturgical experience does not provide an opportunity to exercise this
option. In the setting of the Sunday worship we are confronted
with a number of people all at the same time.

There is no such thing as the perfect instrument for communication, not even for a specific time, place, and community.
Each of them has inherent limitations, and those limitations will
be imposed upon the message in spite of any efforts we might
make. The message itself may be—and in the case of preaching
certainly is—bigger than any instrument of communication or
than any combination of instruments; but nothing more of that
message can be communicated than the instrument of communication can accomodate and convey. This was what Marshall
McLuhan meant (or, at least, part of what he meant) when he
said that the medium is the message; it does not in itself provide the content of the message, but it significantly shapes and
limits that message.

This means that our instruments of communication should be
chosen with great care. In practice they are chosen for a variety
of reasons, or a combination of reasons. It may be that we

choose a particular one by default, as it were—that is, out of habit or because it is the traditional one used. Or, it may be selected simply because it is convenient; being there at hand, it requires less energy, imagination, or expense. Others choose certain techniques because they have developed a skill or talent for working with particular ones, which therefore become more flexible and more susceptible to a variety of messages. Sometimes a particular choice is made because we know from experience, or we suspect, that those with whom we wish to communicate perceive better, more fully, or more comfortably through a particular instrument or a certain combination. We would not knowingly employ means that would so limit and shape the message as to distort it; nor would we deliberately attempt to effect the communication process through instruments that could not be used and appreciated by those with whom we intend communication. Either course would be self-defeating.

Many of our choices are made more or less subconsciously; others are carefully calculated. In either case, our choice of communication tools reflects our perception of our fellow communicants as well as our own perception of the message itself.

Chapter

4

THE PREACHER
AS MEDIUM AS MESSAGE

IN THE 1800s a bill came before the Congress of the United States that would appropriate funds for stringing a telegraph line diagonally across the country from Maine to Texas. At one point in the debate a congressman sought to question the wisdom of such an expenditure by asking: "What if the people in Maine have nothing to say to the people in Texas?" Apparently the congressman was not acquainted with the corollary to Parkinson's Law, which holds that "if a medium is there, we will use it—whether we have anything to say or not."

For better or worse, the sermon is there, and we have seen some of the reasons why it probably will remain there for some time to come. Nowhere is the irrefutability of Parkinson's Law more easily demonstrated. Come Sunday morning, the sermon will be preached—whether we have anything to say or not.

A few years ago a television producer was commissioned by a national denominational office to do a series of dramatized spot announcements designed to stimulate interest in the Gospel message and cause the viewer to think about some of the implications of the Christian message for his own life. Before actually planning the series, the director of the project felt it would be wise to develop a clear statement of just what the Christian message was. It seemed reasonable to him to inquire of professionals; surely the ones above all others who should know the content of the Christian message would be the deans of seminaries. In high expectation, then, although perhaps with some naiveté, he wrote the deans of the seminaries and asked them to please state as succinctly as possible just what the Gospel is.

The producer later shared with me his dismay that most of the responses were informational rather than experiential. He had received some excellent theological statements that undoubtedly could be of great value in a classroom, but to one charged with the development of a series of television spots aimed at reaching millions of nontheologically trained people, they were virtually useless.

Actually, he had made an unreasonable request. What he had asked for was an essay, and that's what he got. What he wanted was a brief sermon, a witness. But an effective preacher doesn't preach in a vacuum. He doesn't preach in "general." Rather, he preaches to a specific congregation in a unique and unrepeatable situation. There simply is no such thing as the Good News in general. The gospel experience is always highly personal, immediate, and specific.

This is not to say that the message is nontheological. Quite the contrary. It must be tested and continually challenged by the most hard-nosed theology we can devise. It is to say that in terms of temporal sequence, the experience of the Good News is not primarily a cognitive one. It is not in itself a theological formulation; it gives rise to theological speculation and leads to formulation. It must meet the test of reason, but it can never be arrived at by reason. It must be experienced and witnessed to. And therein lies one of the preacher's most recalcitrant problems.

Clergy, at least as much as most people, did a lot of kicking and screaming while being dragged reluctantly into the twentieth century by Marshall McLuhan. The idea that the medium is the message is threatening enough to anyone sensitive to its implications, and an already embattled and vulnerable clergy felt keenly the peril that lurked ominously behind the clever phrase. If the medium really is the message, even to the limited extent suggested in the last chapter, and if the preacher really is one of the media chosen by God for the communication of his Good News, then, willy-nilly, the preacher embodies the message itself.

This is a notion that preachers have been trying to reject for centuries. We have never been able to feel comfortable with the idea that preaching was anything more than just a person talking. But our discomfort and our passionate disclaimers may have been based on a misconception. To say that the preacher is the message is not to say that he is the originator of the message—that is quite another thing. Nor is it to say that the preacher is more or less or other than a human creature. Indeed, preaching really is just a man or a woman talking—but it is a person talking about an experience that has actually happened to him, about the authority that experience now has for him, and about the intellectual and ethical implications of that experience. Others have had similar experiences—and one of the goals of preaching is to help those others identify and name and celebrate them—but no one has had that preacher's experience because that experience involved that particular person, and no one else is that person. It is, therefore, his message, and he is responsible for it and to it.

The warden of the College of Preachers in England, D. W. Cleverley Ford, has said that "whether we relish the fact or not, a preacher is listened to in the first place not because of the content of his message, nor because of its attractive form, but because of the [person] who is uttering it." Many years ago Ralph Waldo Emerson exclaimed, "Who you are speaks so loudly I cannot hear what you say to the contrary." And centuries before that, Aristotle had listed the character of the speaker as one of the three primary elements of successful rhetoric, along with genuine concern and sound reasoning.

Generally, the sermon occurs during that part of the liturgy subtitled the "Ministry of the Word." Liturgically, that phrase is used to identify the first part of the eucharistic rite. In popular use, the ministry of the Word means any part of the service, or an entire service, that focuses upon reading Scripture and preaching. Theologically, the phrase is fraught with meaning. As we have noted previously, St John identifies the Word with the Son of God and even uses it as a title. The evangelist stresses the personality of the Word, the divinity of the Word, the creative and salvific power of the Word, and the incarnation of the Word which became flesh.

Whatever else the ministry of the Word might mean, then (and it has many dimensions of meaning), it means at least the ministry of Jesus Christ. One who proclaims the Word proclaims the incarnate God. One who exercises the ministry of the Word exercises the ministry of Christ, bringing into being at that moment, among a particular community, the Christ event. But it is the Christ event as experienced by a particular individual and then filtered through that individual, with all his peculiar physical, mental, and spiritual limitations.

How could this be? How could God dare entrust his precious Word to the distortions and myopia of prejudiced, weak human beings? Well, how else? An old legend has it that when Jesus returned to his heavenly throne, the angels and archangels all gathered around to hear of his adventures on earth. When he finished his story, one of the celestial beings is reported to have asked skeptically, "What kind of plan do you have in case those eleven men fail?" To which the Son of God replied, "We have no alternate plan."

Isn't this the way God has always chosen to reveal himself to his people—through history as interpreted by men and women of his creation? Preachers, of all people, are aware of this mode of revelation. After all, they preach it week in, week out, reminding their listeners that they are the hands and feet of the body of Christ, that they are the real ministers of Christ, that they should so order their lives that their neighbors will be aware of God working in and through them. Yet preachers themselves sometimes have considerable difficulty accepting the implications of this exhortation. I am not here pleading for higher moral and ethical standards on the part of the clergy—although that might be a desirable thing. Rather, I am trying to call attention to the fact that basically the preacher has nothing to proclaim outside of his own experience. It simply is not enough to know *about* God; the preacher must *know* and *be known of* him.

Sooner or later most preachers become acutely aware of this fact, and that discovery then becomes crucial to all the rest of their lives. For those who have in fact experienced and identified the love and forgiveness of God, the judgment and the challenge, the cross and the crown, preaching can suddenly or gradually become a joy and a celebration. For others, unable to identify such a personal experience, preaching becomes a burden. Some of these latter try to fake it—a few may do so successfully for a time, to their own ultimate frustration and destruction. Others try to ignore the clear implications of preaching and revert to oratory, pedagogy, entertainment, or a few muttered phrases off-the-cuff while pleading the inefficacy of preaching in today's world. Some have the courage to quit, which is at least an honest and responsible course.

Most people in the world, including many baptized Christians and some who are ordained, have never experienced the Good News in their own lives, or at least have never identified that experience as such. This is a perfectly acceptable condition —lamentable, no doubt, but acceptable. What is unacceptable— *not* okay—is the attempt to preach out of an experience that one has never had, that is not one's own. Such attempts mock the Word and destroy the man, not to mention the devastating effect they may have on the hearers.

Obviously, I am not referring to one's rhetorical talents or skills. It is regrettable but true that talent and relgious experience are unequally distributed among people; those who have the one frequently do not have the other. In fact, a natural talent for public speaking and a highly developed forensic skill can be a handicap if they mislead one into believing that possession of such a treasure is a sure sign that God has called one to be a preacher. Ironically, such people can give a highly creditable performance which, for quite a long time, can deceive both the preacher and his hearers. If the realization does finally come to the preacher that forensic talent is not the primary prerequisite for effective preaching, the disillusionment may be devastating. Skill is important—much more important than many are willing to admit—but it can be learned. Unfortunately, no diploma, certificate, nor license can provide the only authentic credentials for preaching. Not even the press of a bishop's holy hands is a guarantee.

Preaching is a dangerous enterprise. If the surgeon general of the United States were really on his toes, he would require that every certificate of ordination or license to preach prominently display the legend: Warning: It has been determined that preaching may be hazardous to your health. No one can stand before a congregation week after week, year after year, and talk about the most important, vital, normative thing in his life and not finally be stripped naked. He may not be subject to the legal charge of indecent exposure, but no set of vestments is sufficiently distracting nor voluminous to provide a safe hiding place; no pulpit is high enough nor solid enough to afford adequate protection. Sooner or later, most preachers come to the realization that they have revealed far more of themselves than they had ever intended or wanted to. Here again, the preacher is faced with a decision. Some accept the condition of vulnerability as appropriate to the enterprise, rejoice in it, and live. Some try to find another parish. Some try to find another occupation. Some die.

Surprisingly, not every preacher does recognize just how accurately he has revealed himself, how deeply he has been exposed. It is a pathetic thing to see a preacher who really believes he has been successful at fooling everyone, or almost everyone. He is like the emperor who fondly imagines that his nakedness is covered by raiment of fine spun gold.

Many preachers feel trapped by circumstances. They really did not know what it would be like. If anyone ever told them, which is unlikely, they didn't remember it or didn't believe it, or both. Now they feel intimidated by the requirements of the liturgy, the expectations of their congregations, and their own role definition—not to mention a severly battered ego. Some suspect that they should not preach. A few know that they cannot preach. These live in dread of Sunday morning, sleep briefly and fitfully Saturday night, and breathe a long sigh of relief at noon on Sunday when it's all over for one more week.

What may be one person's disaster, however, is the very definition of life for another. Fortunately many, probably the large majority of preachers, have indeed experienced the love and forgiveness and the sheer joy of Jesus Christ. They not only have something to preach about, they feel compelled to share the Good News with the community and the world. They know their vulnerability and rejoice in it. They are fully aware of the risks and see them as opportunities. Far from feeling trapped, they feel released. To these—probably to you—preaching is less an obligation than a privilege; not a task that must somehow be accomplished every Sunday, but a glorious opportunity to celebrate, to minister, to heal, to become, and to enable others to become. Such preachers are constantly searching for ways to proclaim and communicate the saving Word, and they discover such ways in counseling, teaching, writing, social involvement, and in all their recreation as well as in their "work." They rejoice in the appointment of a sermon within the Sunday liturgy precisely because it provides a peculiar opportunity to share the Good News—an opportunity neither better nor worse than all the others, but different, unique. They always have something "to say to the people of Texas" or anywhere else.

They understand themselves to be the medium and joyfully employ whatever tools they can find to aid in their communication of the message.

And so questions are raised: Which is more important, the medium or the message? Which is more crucial, the fact that we preach or what we preach? The act of preaching or the sermon? The questions might be extended to include the whole of the Sunday worship: Which is more important, the fact that we worship or the Christ event which our liturgy is supposed to celebrate and communicate?

The answers are not to be found in terms of either/or; they can only be a both/and. Certainly the sermon depends upon the Gospel as it is actualized in the life of the preacher; the preacher depends upon that experience for his perception of the message and its meaning. Lacking that, whatever else may happen, there is no sermon. There may be a sound, perceptive lecture, a profoundly moving speech, or an amusing entertainment—all well and good in their place but not the same thing as a sermon, even if delivered in the context of the liturgy.

Likewise, God has chosen to reveal himself through the words of men and women as they identify and interpret his redemptive action in their own lives and in the world, and thereby help us to do the same. As Farmer said: "Christianity is a preached religion." At least in the pragmatic sense of communication, the sermon is as essential to the Gospel as the Gospel is essential to the sermon. The medium is the message is the medium isthemessageisthemediumisthemessageis. . . .

But this cannot be the end of the matter. Recalling our definition of communication and the elliptical model used to diagram that definition, the message and the medium—that is, the Gospel, the preacher, and the sermon—do not complete the communication process. The missing (sometimes literally) and too frequently neglected ingredient is would-be hearers of the Word. And not hearers only, but participants. Preaching requires a congregation.

The preaching event is a personal event—that is, the sermon is preached by a person with the intent and the potential of bringing a person (or several) to The Person. And this can be accomplished only in the context of trust. Trust is an essential ingredient in the process—essential to preaching and proclaiming the word; essential to receiving the Word. Without a congregation to hear and participate, and without the trust necessary to enable that hearing and participation, the sermon ceases to exist and all that is left is a vocal exercise in futility.

Fortunately, there is a predilection toward trust on the part of most Christians. We really *want* to trust our preacher, because we really want to share in and celebrate the Gospel experience. We come with a deep and stubborn longing to hear and to participate. What *Good News* . . . has *God* . . . got for *me* . . . *today?*

Trust is not established by wishing; it is built slowly and painfully by living. The effective preacher is not one who suddenly appears in the pulpit on Sunday morning to preach *to* "his" congregation; but one who lives among and with the congregation and who is able, in all honesty, to identify himself as a member of that worshiping community. True, he is a member with a peculiar role, but then every member has a peculiar role. Trust is not built in an atmosphere of "I and they." It can only survive when the only possible reference is to "us." But it is not enough simply to use first person plural pronouns in the sermon. Any congregation knows immediately and instinctively when the homiletical "we" really means "you." No one is fooled by the words if they know the man; and if they don't know the man, the words don't much matter anyway.

Effective communication calls for mutual participation by all the parties involved. Thus, there is a mutual ownership of the sermon. In the same way, there must be mutual ownership between preacher and congregation—that is, he owns and is owned by the worshiping community. This means that the preacher has a personal investment in the decisions of the community, in its choices and its actions, for he has a stake in its future. He shares that future, and thus shares the present hopes and plans, failures and sufferings, joys and celebrations. In the pulpit on Sunday morning he is the same person he is at a friend's kitchen table on Tuesday, in a town meeting on Wednesday, at a marriage feast on Thursday, at a graveside on Friday. The sermon is a climax toward which all the days and nights have been building. One of our own—a friend whom we trust—is laying himself bare in order that we might hear and participate in the Good News God has for us as a community and for me as an individual—today. And such an act is always a sacred moment, even in church.

Trust and risk are two sides of the same coin. I can only afford risk with those whom I trust. But I learn to trust by risking. And all of this can only be worked out in the process of living. I have known, as I am sure you have, many preachers who, when measured by any of the usual homiletical standards applied by one outside the community, were mediocre at best, but who had been loved by a congregation into being effective Good News-bringers to those people.

This, incidentally, is one of my chief complaints about the procedures so frequently followed by calling committees in those traditions where it is customary for the congregation to hire their clergyman. Sometimes they are even called pulpit committees. An outsider is not usually a good judge of the effectiveness of any preacher's gospelling. Hearing him preach in a neutral place (where he has been invited as a not very subtle subterfuge) or in a congregation looking for a clergyman, more often than not will result in a false, or at least an unreliable impression. Hearing him preach once in the congregation where he belongs is not much better. It would be more helpful to interview members of that congregation. If they were hesitant about sharing information and impressions, that in itself might be a good indicator that they valued the presence of the preacher.

The same principle applies to the practice of having a guest or visiting preacher. As a seminary professor, I receive frequent invitations to preach in some parish or other with which I have no relationship at all beyond a friendship with the rector, if that. Such invitations are flattering and often very tempting— my ego thrives on that kind of stroking. But I know that the best I can hope to do in such a situation is to inform or entertain, or perhaps even stir the emotions of the congregation. Unless it is someone with whom the congregation has some other relationship—one who can in some way be identified as a part of that community and thus have an investment in their lives—I believe that the best that can ever be hoped for with a guest preacher is a stirring performance rather than a true sermon.

Surely there is someone in the congregation who has experienced the Good News of Jesus Christ in his life and who even has some modest skills of communication—someone who really has a stake in that community. Even if a clergyman must be invited to preside at a celebration of the Eucharist, there is still no reason why the preaching could not be done by some member of the worshiping community. Better, I would think an amateur sermon than a professional performance. (Amateur: one who does a thing for the love of it.)

On the other hand, performance is precisely what we have led most Christians to expect on Sunday morning. This is partly the result of two thousand years of preaching characterized by being monological, aural, and visually static. It is partly the result of not recognizing the limitations of that kind of presentation and of not taking advantage of its potentials. But it is more the result of not really having or knowing anything else to do but declaim, entertain, inform, or harangue; that is, perform.

A good performance done by a real artist, whether in the field of vocal or instrumental music, dance, mime, drama, speech, or whatever, is a joy to behold and a delight to hear. A performing artist can move an audience to tears or laughter, arouse anger or fear, titillate or soothe. In the process they may, or they may not, witness to the Good News of the redemptive action of God in Christ. Certainly, such witness is not a criterion for an artistic performance. Furthermore, the idea of a performance carries the connotation of something done by one person (or a select group) to or for the benefit of an audience whose participation is generally passive and vicarious. This certainly does not fit any part of the definition of preaching which we have been gradually constructing.

Unfortunately, it is precisely what is attempted in the name of preaching Sunday after Sunday in parish churches throughout the land. And the most obvious fact about it is that most preachers simply are not very good at it. They just can't compete with the professional artists who perform for us nightly on TV and who can be seen in person so frequently at the theater or in a night club, or even at the circus. Few preachers can match the professional artist in talent; fewer still have devoted the vast amounts of time necessary to perfect the skills displayed by the professional.

Yet, the standards of judgment and comparison are those used for any performance. One place this becomes painfully evident is in the remarks made to the preacher following the service. Whether out of courtesy or in all sincerity, people actually compliment or criticize the preacher on the basis of his *performance*. It was, after all, something *he did*.

Even the architectural setting supports the expectation of a performance. The worship room is usually arranged in fixed rows of seats, all facing the same direction: toward the stage. And a stage is what it resembles more than anything else. Normally, a raised platform, accessible only by steps, bearing perhaps several risers on which important furniture is placed or where important actions occur. Frequently there is a proscenium arch and sometimes a screen of sorts cutting off all or part of the stage from the audience. The lights are brighter on stage than in the house—a normal theater practice, further enhancing the theater-like atmosphere. And it is on this stage that the show takes place. There may be a certain amount of audience participation, but this is carefully controlled and directed and is apparently designed to support the performance as a whole. At the appropriate time and with suitable fanfare, the chief performer, usually identified by a distinctive costume, steps down stage. He may remain front and center, or he may mount a raised platform for which there is a special spotlight. The star is on.

Now, I don't mean to be facetious in this description, much less sarcastic—I am simply trying to describe what it may *look* and *feel* like deep down to a lot more people than would consciously make the connection. Placed in this kind of setting, it seems only natural that the preacher should perform for the audience. It seems natural to both preacher and to the congregation. But everyone knows that the preacher simply cannot compete with the professional performer—even he knows that. So, the expectation is understandably low—on both sides of the pulpit.

It all becomes a vicious circle. The harder the preacher tries to meet the expectation of a performance, the more deeply rooted that expectation becomes on the part of the congregation. And the more convinced they—and he—become that such an expectation is only right and proper, the more he will try to meet it. But the circle *can* be broken. It has been broken in too many parishes now for us ever again to use habit or tradition or ignorance as an excuse.

In all probability, such a reversal will have to originate with the preacher himself; the congregation is usually so conditioned that any possibility beyond that which already exists would be out of the question. But once the process of reversal has begun —in fact, while it is still in the inchoate stage and as a part of the actual beginning—the congregation must begin to assume some active responsibility for the preaching enterprise and for the sermon. I do not mean that members of the congregation must begin to preach. Nor do I mean that they should form a committee to decide what shall be preached about, or how. Rather, they must begin to reassess their role as hearers and active participants in the communication process and in the lived Word.

Just as one who proclaims the Word proclaims the incarnate God and brings the Christ event into being, so one who receives the Word receives Christ himself and participates in that event. There is a famous passage erroneously attributed to St. Augustine wherein the bishop puts failure to listen to preaching on the same level with dropping the Body of Christ at the Eucharist. How many Christian worshipers do you know who accept that kind of responsibility for the preaching event?

There are a good many techniques for helping a congregation exercise this ministry. Some of the best I know of are delineated by William D. Thompson in a little paperback entitled *A Listener's Guide To Preaching* (Nashville: Abingdon Press, 1966). There are many others, and probably those that work the best are those that originate with the people themselves and their own preacher.

Techniques are helpful but they are useful only in a situation where mutual trust already exists, where the preacher is identified by all, including himself, as a member of a particular worshiping community, and where he and they have a pretty clear idea of what a sermon is supposed to be and what might reasonably be expected from it. Or, in a situation where both preacher and congregation are at least willing to learn.

Chapter 5

THE SERMON AS MONOLOG/DIALOG

I AM happy to report that in spite of a bad press, the monological sermon is alive and well in parishes throughout the land. Where it is alive, and certainly wherever it is flourishing, it is due to the fact that the preacher appreciates the unique possibilities inherent in this form of presentation and that he understands and respects its limitations. The health and well-being of the monological sermon is also dependent upon both preacher and congregation having a realistic expectation of the sermon, based upon the clear results of modern communication and learning theory.

If one asks of the classical authors in the field of homiletics— P. T. Forsyth, H. H. Farmer, Phillips Brooks—what sort of expectations one might reasonably have for preaching, the answers will come back in terms of revealing the truth of God in Christ through personal encounter. One searches these authors in vain for a more specific answer in explicit terms. However, the aim of the sermon that is clearly implicit in all their writings is: to induce a change of mind.

Speech theorists would seem to support this goal with such generally accepted propositions as: "Communication may be defined as the eliciting of a response." and "The purpose of all human speech is to effect a change in the listener." On the other hand, one of the most thoroughly demonstrated precepts

41

of learning theory is: A monological presentation is the least adequate of all tools of communication for bringing about attitudinal change.

Educators, theorists, and psychologists have contributed to the research that not only proves this principle but has made it virtually a sine qua non for professionals in almost all fields of communication. Strangely, many preachers and many professors of homiletics have failed to utilize the results of this already mammoth, and still growing, body of research. At least, they have steadfastly refused to acknowledge the implications inherent in it.

The single most constant feature of preaching through the years has been its basically monological character. It is true that from time to time in history (it certainly is not a new phenomenon), preachers have employed many variations of the so-called dialog sermon. Normally, however, this technique has entailed the use of two or more voices to give what is still essentially a monological presentation. Countless other methods of presentation are in use: visual aids, audiovisuals, drama, role play, and dance, to mention but a few. Most of these techniques are not new. Although many of them have been considerably updated by modern electronics, they are still far from common. Even today, with our twentieth-century technology and our increasing understanding of communications theory, a sermon that departs from the monological pattern is considered unusual if not eccentric. Unfortunately, many self-styled avant-garde preachers become so enamored of gimmicks and gadgetry that their presentations tend to become "productions" or "specials" more than genuine sermons.

This sort of overreaction probably is a natural development, and perhaps in the future the sermon will assume a shape now unforeseen. Certainly there is a lot of experimentation going on in this field; some of it is merely capricious, but much of it is being conducted quite responsibly. Nevertheless, for the vast majority of preachers who proclaim the Good News of Jesus Christ week in, week out in parish churches throughout the world, the monological sermon is, and for some time will continue to be, the norm. They have neither the time, the specialized knowledge, nor the unique talents necessary to vary this pattern greatly or frequently.

It is for this majority of preachers and students that this book is written; there is literature aplenty on experimental forms and styles of preaching.

To say that a straight monological presentation is the least adequate instrument by which to effect attitudinal change does not mean that no monological presentation can ever produce *any* attitudinal change—but only that is a poorly designed tool for that purpose. It might work in some instances, but the odds against it are staggering. Used in conjunction with other tools of different design, the odds become much better. Furthermore, there is almost as much evidence for what a monolog *can* do as there is for what it cannot do, and this evidence demonstrates several purposes to which the monolog sermon is ideally suited:

1) It can make explicit for the listener attitudes or knowledge which previously he had held tacitly.

2) It can provide significant positive reinforcement of previously held and acknowledged attitudes.

3) It can help the listener see the implications of attitudes he holds and recognizes as his own.

Undoubtedly there are other functions that can be performed effectively by a monological presentation (such as entertainment and the transmission of information), but the three purposes named have immediate application to preaching. Each of them, singly or in combination, might be realistic goals for the preacher.

Making explicit attitudes and knowledge held tacitly.

Information comes to us from outside ourselves and is acquired through one or more of our physical senses. When information is perceived to be relevant to a particular situation or problem and is, therefore, used in one way or another, a large percentage of it is retained and becomes part of our explicit knowledge. But what happens to the balance—information not perceived as relevant and not used? Some of it may well be irretrievably lost. Some of it is mentally filed for future reference. It is certain that knowledge that has proved useful at any time is never lost entirely. We may say we had "forgotten" about something or other, but what we mean by this is that the information was lying dormant, so to speak. It is not useful to us, of course, until it is recalled by some situation or by something or someone who "reminds" us.

Knowledge is more than sheer raw data. Knowledge also includes schemata by which the data is given appropriate place in our understanding, and a value system by which we measure the truth and usefulness of each piece of information. Much of this aspect of knowledge, too, is tacit. In fact, many philosophers of education hold that all significant knowledge that will ever be available to any individual is held tacitly within that individual. In other words, all of us know not only more than we can say, we know more than we *know* we know. Naturally, we can't act upon knowledge we aren't aware of possessing.

Perhaps even more important for the preacher is the fact that many of our feelings and attitudes are likewise held tacitly. Some of these were formed so long ago and have become so ingrained in us that we no longer recognize them in any explicit way. Others were formed by bits and pieces that we have never really strung together into a comprehensive or useful whole. They are there all right and we can recognize them when they become identified for us; but in the meantime, they remain unarticulated and somewhat below the level of consciousness. These tacit attitudes may or may not be congenial to the intellect, the behavior pattern, or the life-style of the one who holds them. If they do somehow "fit," then making them explicit makes it possible to act upon them consciously and to realize an integrity of attitude and behavior that might not have been possible before. Because this function can, to a great extent, be performed by a monological presentation, the preacher has a rich opportunity to bring about a significant degree of healing in his listeners.

When tacitly held attitudes are not congenial to other, explicitly held, attitudes, to the intellect, or to the behavior pattern of the listener, making them explicit will have the effect of "something's gotta give." Here the preacher should be sensitive to the possibility that the tension thus created may be resolved by different hearers in diametrically opposed ways, and perhaps in ways that the preacher himself would not have wished. It is a risk the preacher must be prepared to take.

The goal here is not attitudinal change but behavioral change. The procedure is to raise to the level of consciousness attitudes that are both desirable and so firmly entrenched that behavior which denies them can no longer be tolerated by the individual. This is the basis of Old Testament prophecy: remember who you are and what you believe to be true, then pattern your behavior accordingly. William Temple once observed that "few radical reformers can hope for great success who are unable to present themselves with perfect honesty as the only true conservatives." Temple, in his typically English way, cited the example of William Wilberforce, who finally succeeded in calling into consciousness the Christian attitudes of Parliament and demonstrating how support of the slave trade was in direct conflict with those attitudes. In this case, the attitudes were strong enough that the behavior simply had to be modified to fit. But there is always the danger that the reverse will be true, and the preacher must be prepared to accept the consequences of the opposite possibility.

Positive reinforcement of consciously held attitudes.

The modern term for this is "peer support." This is an important function of any liturgical celebration and can be accomplished effectively by a monological presentation. All of us need to know that our attitudes are acceptable to others in a community we hold to be significant. We are not speaking here of simple agreement, but of acceptance which does not require or demand agreement. We are talking about basic attitudes that can not only tolerate but even support disagreement.

Attitudinal reinforcement can, in fact, lead to significant behavioral change by providing us with the courage to act in accordance with our convictions. A case in point is the current advertising campaign by the American Heart Association in its efforts to persuade people to give up smoking. One thrust of this campaign is aimed at providing peer group acceptance for the nonsmoker and the former smoker. One who "knows" he should not smoke has this attitude reinforced by his peers and by people whom he admires. Thus, many are given the courage to change their behavior to conform to an already acknowledged attitude.

Drawing out implications of acknowledged attitudes.

The two previously discussed functions of monological preaching lead quite naturally into the third: setting forth clearly the implications of attitudes consciously held, deliberately reinforced, and firmly resolved. In effect, this means the translation of the symbolic liturgical act into everyday behavior. The preacher can perform a key function by showing how this transition can be made. Such concepts as "one loaf," "one body," "one baptism," and "one Lord" have enormous but little realized implications for our daily lives and our personal and political relationships. It seems safe to assume that few Christians have given much thought to the implications of the articles of faith they profess. Even less attention has been given to the implications of the liturgical actions in which they more or less regularly participate.

It is possible for the monological sermon to bring some of these implications nearer to the level of awareness. Here the preacher must be scrupulously honest about spelling out the cost that will be exacted for behavior consistent with Christian belief as reflected in liturgical action. What Christians do and say in the liturgy is just between themselves. When they begin to translate all that into a life-style and behavior pattern in their social and political relationships beyond the Christian community, they must be prepared to pay a high price.

I am personally convinced that this is one of several reasons why so many people in the last decade have become alienated from the Church and why many have separated themselves from it altogether. I really believe many preachers have been doing a better, more honest job of spelling out the cost—and many people simply are unwilling to pay the price. In the past they had become associated with the Church either by default, so to speak, or because they had been sold a bill of goods about sweetness and light. They had been promised something the Gospel never intended: joy without grief, resurrection without the pain of death, a crown without the humility of the cross. Once they got in, and the fine print at the bottom of the page was explained clearly, they rightly felt they had been cheated. The cry went up: "You're changing my religion!" And they were right. Many, unwilling to go along with the change, feeling hurt and betrayed, and believing the price now required to be unreasonable, dropped out.

This is a danger in all liturgy, in all preaching, in all communication. Paul Tillich put forth four possible responses to the Gospel:

1) **One may misunderstand and therefore reject it.** Such a person probably is not a member of the worshiping community. Along with those who have never heard the Gospel in the first place, he represents the primary target for missionary endeavor. If his misunderstanding can be corrected, there is the possibility he will accept the Gospel; but there is another possibility:

2) **One may understand quite well and consciously decide to reject it.** This person undoubtedly is outside the Church. There is always the risk that understanding will lead to deliberate rejection.

3) **One may misunderstand and therefore accept it.** It is with these that the risk is run. If such a person has accepted due to misunderstanding, the probability is that understanding will lead to rejection. But the probability is not a certainty, so the risk must be run. In any case, Christ is not glorified, nor the body of Christ strengthened, by a relationship that is, in effect, based upon a lie.

4) **Ideally, one may understand as thoroughly as he can and in this understanding accept the Gospel and its implications.**

To these possibilities listed by Tillich, I would like to add a fifth: one may partially hear and simply be indifferent. Also, there usually are degrees and mixtures of all these possible responses in each of us. Our chief missionary responsibility lies with those in this last group as well as in the first. But anyone in the first state will certainly not be in a position to be persuaded by preaching, and those in the fifth will probably not.

Our primary liturgical responsibility, and therefore preaching responsibility, lies with the fourth group; and the possibilities open to a monological sermon are well suited to meeting this responsibility. Of course, in the exercise of it we run the risk of alienating those who had accepted the Gospel out of a misunderstanding. But I cannot discover any biblical mandate for successful preaching, only the clear-cut challenge to faithful preaching —probably a more difficult undertaking, and certainly a more threatening and dangerous one.

This list of goals for preaching seems to be severely limited; and, in fact, it is. But to expect of the sermon something it simply is unable to effect, and to continue week after week the preparation of sermons in ignorance or disregard of the inherent limitations is an exercise in futility, frustration, and sin. At the same time, full realization of the potential that does exist for preaching will require the study and application of techniques designed specifically for the goals that monological preaching realistically can aspire to.

Although each of the possibilities discussed above is based upon, and builds upon, the past and the present, they are all definitely and consciously oriented toward the future. Their purpose is to bring new insight into a present situation and to induce change. It has been noted previously that communication theorists say this is the purpose behind all attempts at communication, but there are many different ways of realizing this goal. The monological sermon has its own unique possibilities accompanying its own set of limitations. While these possibilities place some heavy and perhaps strange new demands upon both preacher and congregation, the potential is promising enough to justify the preaching enterprise and efforts at its revision and renewal.

Happily, preaching has something going for it that communication and speech theory does not—indeed, cannot—take into account; namely, the context in which preaching occurs. There are two aspects of this context which extend and enrich the potentiality of preaching beyond the restrictions faced by the monological presentation as conceived by the theorists. One of these aspects is the nature of the community in which preaching takes place and the relationship between the preacher and the community. The other is the event in which preaching occurs and the community's experience of that event.

As stated earlier, most preaching has been, is, and probably will continue for some time to be, monological in its presentation. But note what happens when we posit a worshiping community that acknowledges and assumes responsibility for the preaching event, when we take seriously our definition of communication as that which arises from and is dependent upon mutual interaction, and when the preacher is identified by himself and by others as a member of that community with a stake in its decisions and in its future. In such a context, the sermon may continue to be monological in technique and presentation, but it becomes *dialogical* in nature.

A preacher who understands himself to be a member of a community in which he invests his life and upon whom he depends for the discovery and expression of his personality, unavoidably is in continuing dialog within that community and with its several members. In like manner, the other individual members are part of—contributors to and beneficiaries of—this dialog. By virtue of the interdependence of community and communication, neither the dialog nor participation in it can be avoided even if one should desire to do so. In this setting, the sermon functions as a contribution to the dialog—a unique and significant contribution made to an ongoing process. The sermon does not try to supply all the answers and so shut off all further discussion. Still less is it something altogether outside of and unrelated to the dialog.

The fact that the contribution of the sermon takes the form of a monolog should be neither surprising nor distressing. After all, a dialog is made up of a series of individual monological speeches. Each of these is, or should be, dependent upon what has preceded it. Each speech is made in the light of all that has gone before and with the hope of making a contribution that will, in turn, be a part of future consideration and be taken into account by subsequent speeches. Just so with the sermon. The sermonic statement is not simply laid out there as a discreet and finished product, complete in itself, to be admired, hated, or ignored. The contribution of the sermon, like any other contribution, requires and anticipates the reaction of other members of the community and the enrichment that comes from their affirmations, arguments, questions, and observations.

The preacher strives to make a unique contribution: the Word that could not have been reasoned, that would not have sprung up spontaneously. It cannot—at least not in the worshiping community—be ignored or dismissed, for it provides a dimension not otherwise available. The Word brings the Christ event to bear; it judges, challenges, embraces, heals, redeems. But it does none of these things in isolation—only in community, communication, communion. Whatever the style of presentation, the sermon can and should be dialogical in nature.

In fact, if it is to be effective at all, the sermon will be a part of, and dependent upon, dialog. Any other attempt will result in an experience something like discovering that the manufacturer of a jigsaw puzzle has inadvertently included in the package a piece from an entirely different puzzle. Until he knows this, there is a period of frustration and mounting anger as one seeks desperately and vainly to find a place where the particular configurations and design of the piece will fit. Once it is discovered that the piece doesn't even belong to the puzzle being worked, it is simply discarded (an act perhaps accompanied by a few choice words). On the other hand, the sermon that makes an obvious contribution to the process is like discovering a heretofore overlooked key piece to the puzzle. And the latter experience is as delightful as the former is frustrating.

Once the sermon is seen as dialogical in nature, a whole new array of possibilities is opened up. But there is more. Earlier, the context was said to have two aspects: the community and the event. Even more than the community, the liturgical event in which preaching takes place is something that most speech theory could not be expected to anticipate and take into account. We cannot avoid doing so.

Chapter
6

LITURGICAL PREACHING: 1

ALONG with the community of which he is a member, the most important resource available to the preacher is the liturgy which forms the context of his preaching. Actually, these two elements—worshiping community and liturgy—form a single entity. Each is constituted by the other and dependent upon the other for identity and existence. To the degree that this interdependence is acknowledged by members of the community and is actually operative (as opposed to being theoretical only), liturgy is a perfect example of our concept of communication. Liturgy may be described functionally as *leitourgia* or phenomenologically—as a basic life-symbol.* In either case, the active involvement of the participant/worshiper is paramount. It is obvious that not everyone in the congregation can take a verbal part in preaching the sermon; nevertheless, it is equally apparent that any worship experience which bears the adjective liturgical is under an obligation to involve all the participants experientially.

It will have become apparent by this time that I have been

---

* For an example of the functional definition, see author's *Doing the Eucharist* (Morehouse-Barlow, 1971); for an example of the phenomenological definition, see his *Celebration of Life* (Morehouse-Barlow, 1969).

using the words *"worship," "liturgy,"* and *"sacrament"* some-what loosely and even ambiguously—allowing the reader to make whatever connections between them he will. I must, how-ever, reveal my own bias in order to clarify the terminology of this and succeeding chapters.

It seems clear to me that all (Christian) public worship is liturgical—that is, liturgy-like. I believe the potentialities of preaching can be realized most fully in the richest possible liturgical setting; that is, one which includes a worshiping com-munity self-consciously constituted by and constitutive of the sacramental act. By all odds, the most dramatic, powerful, affec-tive, and effective liturgical symbol possessed by and available to the body of Christ is the full paschal mystery. In its complete-ness, this will include conversion and penitence, fasting and vigil, water-washing and chrismation, the laying-on-of-hands and the kiss of peace, prayers of intercession and thanksgiving, participation in the sacred meal, and acts of unity and fellow-ship. Even Christian communities that seldom if ever celebrate these rites in their fullness continue to identify themselves in terms of this symbol. In other words, the symbol is operative even where unacknowledged.

In practice, most congregations celebrate the paschal myster-ies in their entirety only infrequently. For many, this will be once a year—at the Easter feast from which the rites take their name. A few others will have the opportunity two or, at most, three times a year. But every Sunday—week in, week out—most Christian congregations will deliberately recall the full rites by celebrating the eucharistic feast. One of the principal functions of the eucharistic celebration is to recall for the com-munity the paschal event by which they were formed and from which they receive their identity, and to recall for the individual his own rebirth and incorporation into the body of Christ. Unfor-tunately, many of our liturgical formularies have not been suffi-ciently explicit about this aspect of the Eucharist, so for many it has been chiefly theoretical. Recently, however, the oversight is being corrected. As our formularies catch up to our theology, what had been largely conceptual is becoming experiential once more. It is this inherent characteristic of the Eucharist that makes Christians aware that we are indeed the Easter people. It is this element in the weekly liturgy that makes every Eucharist an Easter feast, every Sunday an Easter celebration. And the proclamation of the Word is an integral part of the paschal event.

Just as all liturgy finds its origin in and takes its identity from the queen of liturgies, just so does all Christian preaching find itself rooted in and ultimately dependent upon the paschal mystery. But it is obvious that not all preaching is self-consciously related to, or even a part of, the liturgical action. For this reason, it seems wise to develop a clear idea of what we mean by liturgical preaching. As we seek to formulate a working definition, two cautions must be borne in mind: (1) the liturgical sermon is not the only type of preaching. In many situations it is not the most desirable; in some it is not even possible. Other types of sermons have their own validity. (2) The parameters for the liturgical sermon are not necessarily the same as those for other types of sermons.

An adequate definition of liturgical preaching is neither as obvious as one might assume nor as simple as many try to make it. The problem is one of exclusion almost as much as it is of inclusion. Certainly the first and most obvious criterion is that liturgical preaching is done within the setting of the liturgy. Acceptance of this criterion says nothing about the validity or efficacy of preaching in a context other than the liturgy; it does insist that liturgical preaching must, by definition, occur within the liturgical action. But not all preaching done, for instance, at a celebration of the Eucharist, can be called liturgical. An adequate definition must be further limiting.

The second necessary characteristic of the liturgical sermon is that it be a biblical sermon. The adjective "biblical" frequently carries with it the connotation of "expository." That usually means something like exegesis and includes a telling or retelling of a portion of Scripture accompanied by a sort of running commentary, placing the story in its historical perspective and then making some application of it for Christians today. This may be a useful technique in some instances, but it certainly is not the only style of preaching that can legitimately be called biblical. A sermon can be thoroughly biblical without ever quoting or referring explicitly to a single verse of Scripture. A biblical sermon will attempt to say what the Bible intends to say—that is, it will seek to proclaim the Good News of what God in Christ has done and is doing; it will proclaim the imminent kingdom of God.

At the same time, a liturgical sermon is surely dependent upon Holy Scripture. The written word of the Bible is a record of the Word of God as transmitted through the events of the history of his people and the response of "men of God" and, supremely, as spoken and done through the human word of Christ. Any contemporary human word that purports to be a response to the Word of God must ultimately find its source in the complete Word as revealed in Christ. Just as bread and wine are merely bread and wine until they are joined unto the Word made flesh and transformed by that joining, so human words are merely human words until they are joined unto, and likewise transformed by, the Word divine made Word incarnate. Theoretically, at least, it would be possible to preach within the context of the liturgy without doing so out of this joining-transforming experience. We make no judgment about such preaching except to say that whatever else it may be, it is not liturgical preaching.

Not all biblical preaching would qualify as liturgical preaching even though done within a liturgical setting. In addition, the sermon must be based upon the liturgical pericopes appointed by the Christian year or the liturgical calendar. This is the most common definition today. It is essentially the operative definition for Reginald H. Fuller in *What Is Liturgical Preaching?* (1957). Professor Fuller is a New Testament scholar by profession, a liturgiologist by avocation, and an Anglican priest by vocation. Given these credentials, it is perhaps inevitable that he should be concerned to promote exegetical preaching based upon the liturgical pericope. And he has plenty of good company.

In his useful book *The Renewal Of Liturgical Preaching*, Professor George M. Bass quotes an essay by a founder of Associated Parishes, one of the foremost organizations for liturgical renewal, in which the clear statement is made: "The sermon should be liturgical, that is, related to the propers of the day." But the same criticism can be leveled at such simple concepts of "preaching the Christian year" as against expository preaching in general. The Christian year is not intended as a system for preaching but, in Dr. Bass's felicitous phrase, as "the celebration of Christ." He further observes that "the preacher is a victim of theological myopia if he perceives nothing more than a system in the Christian year. The Christian year is a proclamation of the essential fullness of the Christian faith in the person of Jesus Christ. Discovering a system for preaching is secondary to acknowledging the basic Christocentricity of the liturgical calendar."

The Christian year is, then, primarily a way of ordering the events in the history of God's people that demonstrates their (and our) proper response to his saving acts. One could, conceivably, preach about these things in the sequence of the Christian year outside the liturgy—although it would seem that to do so would deprive the preacher of one of his principal resources. Likewise, one could preach in the midst of the liturgy without taking either note or advantage of the seasonal emphasis and without any reference whatsoever to the pericopes appointed by the liturgical lectionary. About preaching in either of these cases, we can only say that it is something other than liturgical preaching. And so, we are forced to tighten our definition even further.

Our next criterion is primarily theological. E. H. Schillebeeckx calls attention to the fact that contemporary students of communication stress three aspects of the human word: it has content (that is, something is said), it includes an invitation to response, and it is self-revealing or self-disclosing. When Schillebeeckx looks for these characteristics of the human word as he finds it speaking the Word of God through Jesus Christ, he finds them clearly visible. The Word has as its content the will of God for his people, his saving acts in history and nature. The invitation to respond comes through loud and clear. And, most significantly, Jesus' word reveals the Word that is indistinguishable from God himself and from his acts. By now, the distinctions between content, invitation, and self-disclosure become blurred, so that the word and the Word, the speaking and the act, the incarnation and the God made manifest, blend into aspects of the same thing and are seen as one.

Sacramental theology teaches quite clearly that as the Word is made flesh, so the grace of God is perfected and given in the sacraments. Thus, we begin to see the internal connection between the Word and the sacrament. In fact, they would appear to be so interrelated as to be virtually inseparable. And this is precisely the point made by Schillebeeckx: "Because the sacrament is entirely fruitful only in [one] who receives by faith the gift which Christ makes of himself in the sacrament, the ministry of the word is necessarily directed toward the ministry of the sacrament. What is begun in the word is perfected in the sacrament."

Note especially Schillebeeckx's use of the word "necessarily." This would seem to imply that all preaching that claims to be the Word of God must point unequivocally toward participation in the sacrament. Domenico Grasso, S.J., a professor of catechetics at the pontifical Gregorian University in Rome, stresses the sacramental nature of preaching itself: "Preaching is not only the vehicle through which God makes man aware of His plan of salvation but also a means of grace, a salvific act. It not only announces salvation; it confers it as well."

Lest one think that this is a peculiarly Roman Catholic view, let him read Barth's *The Preaching Of The Gospel* or von Allmen's *Preaching and Congregation* to discover that this is exactly the point of these Protestant theologians as well. Barth insisted that both sermon and sacrament should be part of every Sunday service. He saw the ideal celebration beginning with baptism and concluding with the eucharist, with the sermon acting as a bridge between font and altar. "Only when worship is rightly ordered, with preaching and sacrament, will the liturgy come into its own, for it is only in this way that [preaching] can fulfill its office, which is to lead to the sacraments."

Von Allmen emphasizes that the preaching of the Word always has a sacramental purpose. He writes that the sermon "ever seeks as its end a sacrament which will confirm and seal it. The sermon is not an element in worship which exists for its own sake, but is integral to the structure of the liturgy as a whole."

More recently, Dr. Bass, a Lutheran, has declared that "the sermon demands a response from its hearers so that they may properly celebrate the Eucharist and live in the world as witnesses for Christ." He goes on to say that "the liturgical sermon guards the balance between liturgy and preaching by proclaiming Christ in such a way that the worshipper is led to the altar and the eucharist."

These are not isolated opinions voiced by theologicans removed from the mainstream of Protestant and Roman Catholic thought. On the contrary, they are representative. The relationship between preaching and sacrament is simply too fundamental to be denied even by those whose traditions might in the past have stressed the primacy of either. Since the context in which the Church normally experiences the sacramental ministry is that of the liturgy, the contextual setting for preaching is automatically established. The theological statements quoted above would seem to indicate that the liturgical setting is, or should be, the *only* setting for preaching. However, such a conclusion would be an obvious denial of tradition and experience. We find our theologians hedging their bets on this issue by saying that preaching can, indeed, occur outside the liturgical setting, but they are then forced by their logic to add (by implication if not by explicit statement) that when this is the case, the sermon actually points to fulfillment in the sacrament to be celebrated in a liturgy at some point in the future. Thus, they seem to be saying, all true preaching of the Word of God does point to and find fulfillment in the sacrament, even though the two may be somewhat separated in time. To fall back on such an argument strikes me as diluting the original intent, already made so obvious, to the point that it becomes meaningless.

In addition, many authors apparently would have to say that all preaching about the sacraments, or that refers to the sacraments, is liturgical. Again, such a stance renders any distinction virtually useless. To preach about the sacraments *without* the sacraments is to posit a false distinction between the Word and the act or to collapse the two into a single category in such a way as to say that either is sufficient without the other. The whole point of the preceding theological argument was to demonstrate that either position would be intolerable.

So, while recognizing the efficacy of preaching done outside the liturgy and with no reference to the sacramental action, we must acknowledge as well that not all preaching done within the liturgical context has the goal of drawing the baptized to the Eucharist and perfecting in the sacrament what is begun in the Word. Without forming any judgments about such preaching, we must nevertheless restrict our definition of liturgical preaching to include a self-conscious relationship to the sacrament itself.

Now, what have we so far? Perhaps it would be well to pause at this point and see what sort of a definition is emerging from our examination. An outline of the several criteria, inclusive and exclusive, would look something like this:

(1) **A liturgical sermon is preached within and as part of the context of the liturgy.** But not all preaching in a liturgical setting is therefore liturgical; and the word "context" is deliberately chosen over "setting" as being a more inclusive term.

(2) **A liturgical sermon is biblical in the deepest sense; that is to say, it seeks to proclaim the Good News of what God in Christ has done and is doing—the imminent kingdom of God.** But not all preaching on a scriptural text is therefore liturgical.

(3) **A liturgical sermon grows out of the pericope pertinent to the season of the Christian year and takes full advantage of the emphasis of the season for the celebration of Christ.** But not all preaching on the proper Bible lessons or on the subject of the Christian year is therefore liturgical.

(4) **A liturgical sermon bridges font and altar, leads the worshipers to communion, and culminates in the Eucharist.** But not all preaching about the sacraments or preaching that refers specifically to baptism or to the Eucharist is therefore liturgical.

So far, so good. But surely there is an essential element still missing. Because of the positive/negative aspect of each of the criteria established so far, a given sermon might meet the requirements of them all and yet fail to qualify as a liturgical sermon. Of course, one might say that the final test is meeting all four of the above, but that would be too easy. More importantly, it would eliminate the single ingredient common to all preaching that legitimately carries the description "liturgical."

Chapter
7

LITURGICAL PREACHING: 2

Every organized being forms a whole, a unique and closed system, of which all parts mutually correspond and cooperate by reciprocal action for the same definite end. None of these parts can change without the others changing also; consequently each of them taken separately represents and postulates all the others.

M. CUVIER

The criteria for a liturgical sermon set forth in the preceding chapter are not new nor original. Others, principally Dr. George M. Bass, have formulated similar statements. However, I would like to propose an additional factor, one that carries even Dr. Bass's admirable analysis a step further and that I believe to be determinative for the definition:

The liturgical sermon is an integral part of the liturgical act itself and performs a truly liturgical function. That is, it has a fixed role in the liturgy in much the same way that the Gloria in excelsis, the Creed, the Sanctus, and the Lord's Prayer have fixed liturgical roles. And further, the genuinely liturgical sermon is of a piece with the whole liturgical act.

Of course, it is based upon the Gospel pericope. And, of course, it leads to the altar and the Eucharist. But more than this, it is seen to be not merely a transition between Word and sacrament, certainly not as a hiatus, but as an integral part of

61

the action. There should be no sense of a break in the service—either visually, audibly, or aesthetically—for the purpose of preaching. A change of pace, a different focus, a different tool of communication—all these, yes, presented in such a way that they are seen as contributing to the single liturgical experience. The sermon complements and serves the liturgy just as an offertory procession, the fraction, or the exchange of the peace does. However, a sermon is a very personal act. The Word, the act, and the person are all aspects of a single entity. Unlike a fixed liturgical text, therefore, the sermon is a variable. It is spoken to a peculiar and irreplacable community of specific people in a unique and unrepeatable situation. In the sermon, traditional texts of Scripture and liturgy are given contemporary life and expression. The liturgical sermon is an art form in itself which has meaning and identity only when set within a larger art form, just as, for instance, the music of the liturgy.

Up to this point, establishing the grounds for our criteria has been easy. When it comes to this final, determinative element, we find little or no precedent, especially with regard to any theological base. This is due in part to the fact that the criterion itself is one not commonly applied. In another part, it is probably due to the fact that many who concern themselves with preaching are either biblical scholars, theologians, or homileticians who claim no real competence in the field of liturgy. If they were to give this point any attention at all, they probably would tend to classify it as a matter of preference, taste, or personal style. (There are notable exceptions to this generalization—Professor Reginald Fuller, for instance.)

To the contrary, I believe this criterion has a theological basis every bit as sound as those we have discussed. Again, it is Schillebeeckx who gives us the best clue when he says: "The ministry of the word is not something merely prefacing the administration of the sacrament, but rather penetrates to the very heart of the sacrament's celebration." Just as the prophetic Word called forth and interpreted the historical events of salvation by virtue of being a Word of God under a human form, liturgical preaching brings to light Christ's saving work in the sacrament. In liturgical preaching a ritual act becomes the mysterious manifestation of the divine act of Christ. By human words we proclaim and recall the death and resurrection of Christ; and by these words, as much as by the actions themselves, Christ is re-presented to us. Christ is already present in the pro-anaphora—in the community assembled which prays and professes its faith, in the reading of the Scriptures, and in the liturgical sermon. In Schillebeeckx's words: "The eucharistic celebration is *essentially* a ministry of the word." Indeed, every sacrament is introduced, conferred, and concluded by the ministry of the word. Liturgical preaching, then, necessarily culminates in what constitutes the Eucharist as Eucharist and gives its form to the whole liturgical action: the Word of God made flesh.

The four elements of a liturgical celebration—the rite, the action, the preaching, and the sacrament—are therefore seen to be a single, unified whole. It follows that they must complement one another if the integrity of the whole is to be maintained. It would not only appear incongrous, it would be bad theology to recite a classical liturgical rite while performing some totally inappropriate act—say, while painting the walls of the parish house. Now, it might be that the parish house walls need painting and that, when done as a loving gesture by members of the congregation, the act could be one of offering, prayer, and thanksgiving. Nonetheless, such an act has its own validity and integrity—perhaps even its own rites and ceremonies. To say that it is, per se, apposite to the eucharistic liturgy is to deny the inherent value in both things and to make nonsense of the liturgy of the Lord's Table. In the same way, one could not imagine celebrating the baptismal liturgy in every particular until it came time for the administration of the sacramental element and then, instead of water-washing the candidates, feeding them bread and wine. The rites simply would not match up with the ceremonies.

Note the quotation with which we began this chapter. It was taken not from a liturgist or a preacher, but from the works of a medical researcher—in 1821! When M. Cuvier speaks of "every organized being," he is thinking in biological terms. We hope that the liturgy qualifies as an organized expression of an organized being: the body of Christ. Cuvier's point is precisely my own. When the liturgy is seen as a whole, the role of liturgical preaching becomes something other than merely a sermon preceding the sacrament or injected into the rite at some point. The sacrament is the embodiment of the Word, the rite pronounces the Word, and the liturgical performance is the Word (and man's response to it) enacted. It is the same Word that is pronounced, embodied, and enacted, and the very act of pronouncing the Word of God is tantamount to its embodiment and its enactment. All are interdependent and each is integral to the whole.

When the preacher fails to take this into account, when the sermon is not really at one with the liturgy, the liturgy wins. So powerful is the liturgical symbol that it will out-shout the sermon. Remember Emerson? "Who you are speaks so loudly I cannot hear what you say to the contrary."

Several years ago I heard a faculty colleague preach at a local parish. The theme of the sermon was the freedom that Christian faith brings, the discovery of one's self that can result within such freedom, and the joy of knowing one is accepted by God as a unique individual rather than as an automaton responding mechanically to rules and rubrics. It was a good sermon. My friend had done his homework well, and he was obviously a living, joyful example of the kind of freedom he proclaimed. But he had reckoned without the liturgy. It belonged to a former time, another people, a different culture. The presiding priest moved and spoke mechanically and stiffly. The music was pedestrian. The environment seemed to press one down. The whole thing was dull, drab, and joyless; but mainly, it was rigid. It completely denied the concept of freedom so well put forth in the sermon. And the liturgy won—the sermon was obviously a lie.

Another friend, ministering to a congregation in Hawaii, began early one week to prepare his sermon for the following Sunday. He discovered that all the appointed Scripture stressed the theme: "Rejoice in the Lord." Being a joyful person himself, he had high hopes for the sermon and began his preparation with enthusiasm. To his surprise, he found it difficult, until he suddenly discovered the root of the problem: it was the liturgy. "I just couldn't preach a rejoice sermon in the midst of that same old worship service that exhibited little or no joy anywhere else." So, he talked about it with two or three people, soon a dozen or more were involved. They felt that one of the key elements would be music, so they selected songs from a new hymnal—one with bright, modern tunes and contemporary imagery. Unfamiliar songs required a congregational rehearsal, and they decided to do this outside the church, on the *lanai* (porch), where the people would normally gather anyway. This, in turn, called for special instrumentation. They ended up with a couple of guitars, accordians, ukuleles, flutes, and so forth. As the congregation arrived, they were caught up in the music and joined in the singing, even while greeting one another. After awhile—not at any prearranged time, but when everyone seemed to be ready—they all processed into the church singing; and the balance of the service went on in the same tone. The preacher reported that as he greeted people after the service, "they had the same names, but different faces. They really seemed to be new people. Something had happened to them." What had happened, of course, was an authentic liturgical experience. And the liturgical sermon was *there!* Why must it be so rare as to be noteworthy?

That the sermon should aim at being an integral part of the liturgical action does not mean that it must be bland or undistinguished. I certainly do not intend to rule out the possibility—indeed, the hope—of excitement, surprise, and even shock.

The liturgy as a whole should be an exciting experience, and none of its several components is intended to be dull or altogether predictable. In fulfilling its liturgical role, the sermon participates in, and contributes to, the enthusiasm, the passion, and the sensuality of the liturgical celebration.

From the list of possibilities for monological preaching reviewed in Chapter Five, it is clear that the monological sermon has a greater chance to be effective if it does not stand alone but is confirmed by the full liturgical action. The liturgy provides precisely the symbol needed to bring tacit knowledge to the level of awareness. As the sermon interprets the symbol and the action, the meaning of both symbol and that which is symbolized becomes more apparent. Christ *is* present in the baptized community, and the Word of God is deeply and inextricably imbedded in each of its members. As in a piano, the strings are already provided; it remains for the "men of God" to strike the chords that will set those strings vibrating. The Word does not come to the baptized as something totally foreign to his nature or his knowledge, but as something that resonates with what he already knows and is.

It has already been pointed out that the liturgy provides community support for a certain range of attitudes and behavior. In fact, in the liturgy we verbalize and physically enact the very behavior and attitudes we are most desirous of having reinforced. Furthermore, the Word is not merely that which is spoken, but it is the act and the very life of the speaker. Word and act are two ways of looking at the same reality, and the liturgical sermon can both demonstrate and encourage this integrity.

Finally, in spelling out the implications of our recognized attitudes, the preacher is talking about cost—in theological terms, the cross. But he cannot, he dare not, stop there. We are already afraid of the cost, and if it proves to be too high (as we already suspect), we simply cannot afford it and will have to forego whatever benefits might be promised. The whole project becomes just too expensive. It is the unique function of the liturgical preacher to tell us how we *can* afford it. Not only can he tell us, he can demonstrate it in the liturgy itself. This is one of the things the whole liturgical action is designed to do, and the sermon is an integral part of that action.

To speak the Word is to project into the future. It is to call the future into being. The decisions, the actions, and the words of the people of God, having the force of the Word of God, have eternal significance. As the three persons of the godhead are theologically distinguishable but inseparable, so the Word and the Spirit are one. It is characteristic of the Spirit that it moves forward and moves with freedom. The acts appropriate to the Word are costly, but in the unity of the Word and act there is healing and wholeness and freedom.

Just as the liturgy is designed to incorporate action, rite, and sacrament, so is it designed to incorporate a sermon. The reverse is true as well; that is, the liturgical sermon is designed deliberately to fit into the total experience which includes rite, ceremony, furniture, architecture, music, action, and a particular community with its own peculiar way of being and doing. It would be a grave mistake to think of the liturgy primarily as providing support for the sermon. Also, the sermon must not be looked upon chiefly as an adjunct to the liturgy. It is only together that the integral whole is formed. When both liturgy and sermon are designed and executed with this essential interdependency in mind, the omission of either becomes impossible, and the peculiar definition of liturgical preaching being proposed is seen to be not only appropriate, but necessary.

We can now put our final criterion in a form to match that of the previous four:

A liturgical sermon is an integral part of the liturgical act. Probably this could not be so unless the four preceding criteria were also met. Therefore, all preaching that meets this criterion would be defined as liturgical.

All these criteria can be summarized in a single statement:

A liturgical sermon is one which is thoroughly biblical; which takes full advantage of the Christian year and the appropriate pericope; and which is an integral part of the liturgical action, leading the baptized to fulfillment in the Eucharist.

The temptation now is to say: "Well, there it is. Now, go preach." Theoretically (and in literary form), the above is an absolute statement of an absolute definition. In practice, it's quite another matter. Frequently—more often than most of us would care to admit—with full appreciation of all the elements involved and with all the criteria firmly fixed in our minds, the whole thing just seems to fall flat. At other times, apparently following the same procedures, everything falls into place, and it all clicks. Most often, our efforts result in something somewhere between dismal failure and exhilarating success.

Fortunately, there are some things we can do to tip the scales in our favor. They will not insure success, nor will they guarantee against failure, but they can go a long way toward facilitating the preaching enterprise. These will be the subject of the remaining chapters of this book. Let us not lose sight, however, of the fact mentioned earlier: success is not required of us—faithfulness is. That faithfulness has several different aspects: faithfulness to God and his Word, to the record of that Word as interpreted by the "men of God," to the liturgy and the Church, to the particular congregation and their unique situation, and to oneself. Keeping all those balls in the air at once is both difficult and risky. But the preacher who is clear himself about the cost, and about how *he* can afford it, can effectively and joyfully preach the "uncomfortable Gospel."

PART TWO

Getting It All Together

Competence in preaching is not an automatic by-product of theological education or of readiness to serve the Church—important as both obviously are. Neither exuberance of subject matter nor solicitude for the congregation is enough.

To convert talent into the skill that distinguishes a proficient preacher requires knowledge, discipline, and imagination. It calls for fortitude and industry.

Dale E. Bussis

Chapter
8
"GOSPELLING"

"WE REALLY think a lot of our pastor. In the first place, he's a fine person, but beyond that he knows how to get along with people. He has a talent for getting participation in the church's program by all age groups. I guess he's pretty good as an administrator—things seem to run pretty smoothly, and he's a terrific teacher and an expert at counseling people when they're in trouble or anything. Of course, he's not such great shakes as a preacher, but after all . . ."

This is an assessment one hears in parishes all over the land, and it probably squares very well with the pastor's own self-image. If one as obviously gifted and as well respected as this is not "such great shakes as a preacher," it can only be for one of two reasons: either he doesn't want to be or he has never been taught how, or both. Not everyone can be talented, but anyone can learn to be competent. Yet many clergy, devoted to their calling and firm in their commitment to Christ, place preaching relatively low on their list of priorities. Others recognize well enough the importance of preaching but have never had adequate training and somehow haven't been able to "get it all together" on their own.

Many seminaries have recently enriched their homiletics curriculum and have recognized that preaching is a discipline in its own right and can be learned. While talent cannot be learned, the talented can learn to develop and utilize their gifts, and those without natural abilities can discover facilities they were previously unaware of, learn new skills, and with perseverance can become effective Good-News-bringers to their congregations.

Frequently the task begins with unlearning: old attitudes must sometimes be cleared away to make room for positive new ones. My colleague and frequent "partner in crime," Dr. Donald F. Chatfield of Garrett-Evangelical Theological Seminary in Evanston, begins a course in preaching by assuring the students that they don't really have to preach badly. Poor preaching, he says, is

. . . an acquired skill, like sloppy handwriting or porcine eating habits. Bad preaching is learned from skilled mentors. These preachers have put in a lifetime practicing to be dull. It takes practice to take the most exciting religion in the world and put people to sleep with it. Most bad preachers grew up under bad preachers, which explains why they know with such startling precision how to preach badly. The beginner in any profession is tempted to imitate the men of that profession with whom he is most familiar. The imitation is unconscious, and so all the more difficult to root out. Your preaching need not be an unknowing mime of your past masters, however. Part of the process of emancipation is a matter of replacing bad habits with good skills. Part of it is learning who you are and what your communication strengths and weaknesses are. But the most important part is getting a strong hold on what the Gospel is, and what it means to you."

Homiletical theory alone will not make a preacher. Any set of principles, such as those set forth in this book, will help only as they are acted upon. Instruction, no matter how meticulously tailored for the particular individual and his or her specific situation, will avail only when put into practice. One of Charles Schultz's cartoon panels depicts Charlie Brown disconsolately dragging his baseball bat and mitt behind him while muttering aloud: "A hundred and thirty-eight to nothing. How can anyone lose a hundred and thirty-eight to nothing when they're so sincere?" Sincerity, while essential to preaching, is no substitute for skills painfully acquired and constantly practiced.

Preaching takes time. It takes time to learn, and it takes time to do. Nor does that time diminish through the years. Many fledgling preachers are appalled to discover that those who appear to have more talent, and who clearly have a great many more years of experience, spend even more time on their preparation than the novice. Of course, the time is differently distributed, that is, the bulk of it is spent in different ways by the more experienced, more talented preacher, but the total amount of time devoted to the preaching enterprise is apt to be greater rather than less. Where do they find the time? Well, of course, it is chiefly a matter of ordering priorities. Somehow, the busiest people find time to do the things they really believe to be the most important. They may complain that they never have time for the things they really want to do, but usually this is a thinly disguised subterfuge; they are, in fact, doing what they most want to do.

The first part of this book was devoted to demonstrating the imperative for good preaching imposed by theology, by pastoral considerations, and by one's sense of liturgy as well as by an awareness of the requirements of faithful stewardship. I offer no gimmicks or shortcuts for meeting that imperative. I don't know any. On the contrary, what will be offered assumes a commitment on the part of the preacher to respond to the challenges and utilize the resources of the context of preaching as set forth earlier. Only then will what follows make sense. In the preparation of his sermons, the two greatest resources available to the preacher are his own time and the community in which he ministers.

But let me once again warn the unwary of the danger. Undoubtedly, the orientation I am suggesting for preaching in general, and for liturgical preaching in particular, is a hazardous course for the preacher to adopt because of its high probability of being *effective*. There is an old joke about the parishioner who complained that his pastor had "quit preachin' and gone to meddlin'." To those aspiring to high political office, Harry S Truman once offered the advice: "If you can't stand the heat, stay out of the kitchen." The faithful preacher is one who is willing to run the risk of personal vulnerability, of being taken seriously and forced to live with the implications of his preaching. One may live a long and happy life, acclaimed by peers, parishioners, and ecclesiastical authorities—perhaps even be elected a bishop—without ever attempting the uncomfortable Gospel. In fact, to do so might even be a surefire guarantee against such universal acclamation and ecclesiastical promotion.

For those who are game, then, let's explore some ways that the principles discussed might be put into action. As the first step, let's be clear about the purpose of preaching in the first place. Apart from responding to general theological considerations, rubrical directions, and traditional practice, what does the preacher intend to be doing? Surely it is to bring the Word, the Good News, the Gospel to bear upon a specific situation within a specific community of specific people—to communicate the saving Word. This Word is not at all ambiguous, but it is paradoxical: it judges and does not condemn; it demands commitment and bestows freedom; it elicits pain and results in healing; it promises death and grants life. To keep men and women alive in and by the Living Word—that is the role of the preacher.

The word Gospel, which we usually use as a noun, originally was a verb. The purpose of preaching, then, is "to gospel." This is what makes Christian preaching unique among all other forms of public speaking. It is something that could not necessarily be done by the president of a civic club or by a scoutmaster; it is something more than might be expected from a Confucius, an Omar Khayyam, or a Kahlil Gibran. It is more than wise teaching, although the listener may well learn from it. It is something other than moral exhortation, although one may be led by it to examine his conscience and to alter his behavior accordingly. There is certainly a place for good sound teaching, and we all require that our ethics be called into question and challenged; and some of both of these may easily and appropriately occur through liturgical preaching. Neither one, however, is the primary purpose of gospelling; and gospelling is what liturgical preaching is all about.

As a member of your worshiping community, I come on Sunday morning hurting, seeking, needing. I come asking: Is there any word from God? Today? For me? That word might be difficult or comforting, it might be challenging or supporting; most probably it will be some of all these. But whatever character it may take, I need to know that it is from God—he alone is the definition and source of good. I long to know that it is for me personally, not some generalization for "all men." And I must know that it is news for today, not some old back issue dug out of the archives and hastily dusted off. Unless I can be sure of these things, unless this is the word you speak to me this morning, the service may be informative or inspiring or amusing, but I will leave without being touched at the center of my life; still hurting, still seeking, still needing.

Let's take another example. If I go to a physician with a sore elbow or with a bellyache, almost the first thing he does is try to touch me where it hurts. He touches me gently so I won't go through the ceiling or become galvanized by pain, but he touches definitely. My cry of, "Ow! That's it all right!" is reassuring. Now I know that the doctor knows exactly where I hurt; he'll be working on the right thing. The next step is to give my hurt a name—actually, not the hurt itself, but the cause of the hurt. He won't say: "You have a swollen elbow," or "you have a bellyache." I already know that. Instead, out of his own experience and knowledge, and based upon an examination and testing of me, he will name the root, the source of my hurt. Now, I know that he not only knows where I hurt, but why. And thus, avenues are open for alleviating my pain. The therapy may be as painful or distasteful as the symptoms, but now there is a purpose behind my discomfort: healing. And that's what I came for.

The preacher can follow a similar procedure. First, touch where I hurt—gently, but definitely—so that we both know we're talking about the same thing. Then don't waste too much time on my symptoms. Get down to the issues—quickly. Here the medical metaphor may break down. Once the physician has made his diagnosis, the therapy frequently is quite simple. Not so with preaching. There is always the danger of spending virtually all the sermon time on diagnosis and leaving little or no time for therapy. Unlike the physician, the preacher finds diagnosis fairly easy and lots of fun to talk about. He has no difficulty at all spending fifteen minutes or so eloquently describing the situation—all the while saying very little that I didn't already know even though I might not be so articulate about it. The same preacher may find it difficult to dwell for more than a minute or two on possibilities for alleviating the pain and helping me to see how I can be made well and why the therapy is worth the cost. But that's what I came for.

It is the Word of God, manifest in Christ and alive in the Holy Spirit today that makes Christian preaching unique. Others may have wisdom, knowledge, and sound advice—practical and moral—but only the Christian sermon can proclaim the Good News of Christ. We dare not waste those precious few minutes on Sunday morning trying to do that which is just as well being done by others or in other situations. This is the single opportunity to do that which cannot be done elsewhere.

The story is told of the great Charlemagne that one weekend he found himself and his entourage camped on the outskirts of a town he had never visited. On Sunday morning, the king decided to forego the Mass that would be celebrated in the royal camp by his own chaplain and, instead, to attend services in the parish church nearby. The visitors arrived at the church with no advance announcement and a minimum of fanfare. Upon discovering that the emperor had honored his church that morning, the vicar was beside himself. Setting aside the sermon he had prepared, he delivered a stirring tribute to the wisdom, leadership, and benevolence of the monarch. The following day the preacher received a package by special messenger. It contained a handsome carved crucifix and a note written and signed by Charlemagne himself: "Please mount this on a wall facing the pulpit so that the preacher will never again forget the proper subject of a Christian sermon."

The Christian preacher never has to ask himself: What shall I preach about next Sunday? Week in and week out he preaches Christ: crucified, resurrected, and present in his body. But doesn't it get awfully boring, saying the same thing Sunday after Sunday? Boring? How can it get boring when one is speaking of the most exciting thing in his life? When he is, in fact, talking about the very definition of his life? Surely, I, as the listener, cannot be bored when the preacher is speaking of the most important, the most vital thing I know: my life—how I can have it and can afford to live it. One simply does not get bored with the feel of good bread and with the words, "This is my body." Nothing is less boring than the taste of wine from the cup of salvation. The Word that is broken in the form of bread and shared with the hungry is the same Word that is broken in the form of the sermon and shared with the starving. Bored? Who gets bored with the very bread of life?

John Ruskin once defined the opportunity to preach as "thirty minutes to raise the dead." The expression certainly is dramatic; it is just as certainly mistaken. I'm not dead yet. I may look dead, even act dead, but there's life in the ole boy after all. Your mission "—should you accept it—" is to find that life and stir it; discover that spark and blow on it. Keep me alive, preacher, in the Word that lives! Thirty minutes—preferably fewer—to heal the sick. Fewer than thirty minutes to stir the living. That's your challenge, preacher, your responsibility and your privilege, your cross and your crown. It's a lofty goal, but to aim for less is to admit that your God is too small, and to settle for death—yours as well as mine. To reach for it is to proclaim the God of life. To attain it is to bring healing and wholeness. That's *really* Good News! And *that's* what I came for!

Chapter

9

THE CELEBRATION OF HEALTH

NOT EVERYONE who participates in the liturgy comes hurting, and it would be a mistake to believe that this is the only attitude appropriate or even possible for the Christian worshiper. It is, however, a common assumption. We have been indelibly imbued with the aphorism that "the church is a hospital for sinners." While this maxim contains a good deal of truth, strict application of it can lead to some rather bizarre practices. After all, a hospital is designed to deal with the sick. Well people are denied admission and the sick are sent home as soon as they have attained at least the beginnings of health. If the Church is to live up to its own image as a hospital, and still retain its membership, it must convince people that they are ill. Thus, we seem to spend an inordinate amount of time trying to persuade reasonably healthy, happy people that they really are on the verge of collapse and that anyone in their state should feel terrible. The only place they have any hope for a cure is in our hospital. Strangely enough, once they are admitted we tell them that they can never be cured. There are precious few occasions for celebrating health. Instead, Sunday after Sunday we feel constrained to confirm their sickness and hint darkly of disturbing complications. Such a practice would be in violation

79

of any set of medical ethics, but clerical ethics seems to accommodate it and even encourage it.

My mother, bless her heart, possessed a great deal of folk wisdom—as seems to be the way with mothers. Much of it was quite sound, but I'm afraid some of it is now open to question. She was firmly convinced that if the medicine didn't taste bad it couldn't be doing any good. One of the potions she was determined to consume regularly for the health of body and soul was church-on-Sunday. She frowned upon cushioned pews and overly padded kneelers on the grounds that one was supposed to be uncomfortable in church. Although it was perfectly appropriate for the physical surroundings to be rich, even ornate, and certainly well cared for, the content of the service itself was the more appreciated the more it confirmed her ill health, especially in the area of her own guilt. (Incidentally, the optimum dosage of this bitter nostrum was exactly sixty minutes; every minute beyond was actually counter productive.)

Mother had a lot of good company. Thousands of people feel that their worship experience is not entirely satisfactory unless they have been made to feel pain and become more acutely aware of their burdensome guilt. There are plenty of preachers willing to satisfy their expectations.

It is, of course, true that all of us sin, that our sin prevents us from being whole persons perfectly at one with God and with our fellow human beings, and that this lack of wholeness means that none of us enjoys perfect health. Furthermore, while sin has a corporate as well as an individual dimension, each of us is accountable for our own decisions and each of us bears the burden of responsibility—guilt—for both individual and corporate alienation. But the General Confession that laments: "there is *no* health in us" somewhat overstates the case. There *is* health in each of us—frequently unrecognized, often denied, never perfect, but nevertheless ineradicable. In the eucharistic liturgy we celebrate this gift of health and new life.

Not too long ago I had occasion to visit a children's orthopedic ward in a large hospital. I was surprised to see the vast room festooned with gaily colored crepe paper and balloons, and all the children, even the nurses, wearing bright paper party hats. I asked a nurse what was going on, and she replied that one of the small patients who had been crippled from birth had taken her first unaided step the day before. "She'll be walking soon, and we're all celebrating with her." A celebration of health. For this little girl, it was only the beginning of a long road that would be filled with pain and frustration and heartbreak, and the result would never be perfect health. But it was a momentous event: her first faltering step alone. The child was radiant with pride and joy. She had no need of someone to point out that she was still a cripple. She, better than anyone else, knew full well how much it hurt. What she needed now was just what she was getting: a party with her friends to celebrate the gift that was hers, but which she was just beginning to learn to use.

If the Church is to be regarded as a hospital for sinners, let us at least learn to celebrate the gift of health and new life. The proper focus of liturgical preaching is not pain and death, but healing and resurrection. Our pain is serious, our malady crippling—but it is not fatal!

Saying to someone: "I forgive you, my friend," when he is totally unaware of having done you any harm and of needing your forgiveness, is almost certain to arouse anger. Such inappropriate forgiveness becomes an offense in itself. Forgiveness can be appropriated in a creative or recreative manner only when the offender acknowledges his need for it. And so, it is a thin and precarious line which the preacher walks. On the one hand, the sermon is a part of the thanksgiving celebration for the gift of life and health, and certainly it must reflect the joy as well as the obligations of receiving such a gift. On the other hand, the gift can be received and appropriated only insofar as the intended recipients acknowledge their own individual and collective need for it. When they can do this, its full value can be appreciated. The preacher has the essential role of raising that need to the level of consciousness; and this is more easily done than many preachers suspect. If it is not already fully exposed, it lies just beneath the flimsiest and most transparent of coverings, and usually only the lightest touch is needed to lay it bare.

In preaching, it is perfectly legitimate to use my conscience as a map, but it is illegitimate (and futile) to use it as a whip to beat me with. Sometimes we preachers deepen and intensify guilt in our listeners by whipping them quite unintentionally, but very effectively. One of the chief ways we do this is by incessant harping upon various moral imperatives that we have somehow attached firmly to our understanding of the Christian life and which we seem to believe no one else will know about unless we tell them over and over and over. A pulpit is not intended to be a platform from which one person, even one who is ordained, berates a community of people with "oughts." Time and again, I am told what I *ought* to do. I *know* I ought to give up smoking, take up jogging, go on a diet, love God, love my neighbor; that I should increase my pledge to the church, learn humility, work for the welfare of all people; that I must sell all I have and give it to the poor. I have known most of these things for most of my life. The problem is that I can't *do* them, or at least I don't know how I can afford to do them.

A human conscience is, of course, subject to growth and to increased sensitivity. A conscience can be taught. It is also true that a conscience grows progressively—that is, each new element is dependent upon what already exists. To continue to add new elements before the previous ones have become assimilated and made an integral part of the whole is to risk destroying the entire fragile system, or at least rendering it null and useless. Most of us are already afflicted with consciences which outstrip our performance. Very few Christians need to be instructed about how they *ought* to believe, behave, or feel— what we desperately need to know is how we can translate the oughts we already have into realities. Mark Twain once observed that a lot of people seemed to have trouble accepting those parts of the Bible they couldn't understand; but he confessed that "it isn't the parts I don't understand that bother me —what I have trouble with is all those parts I do understand . . . only too well."

This is precisely the dilemma of most of us. When the preacher belabors us with oughts, he confirms us in our guilt and thereby causes us to improve our defences and strengthen our resistance. When dealing with a physiological malady we know the limitations of the moral imprecation method. One doesn't tell a starving man that he ought to eat or a sick man that he ought to get well. We minister to the starving by showing them where food is to be had and how they can get it, and to the sick by showing them what therapy is available and how they can acquire it. We know that it's a waste of time to tell an alcoholic that he ought to give up drinking. No one is more aware of this than he himself. Sure, he ought to give up drinking; he even *wants* to give up drinking. The question is: How? How is he able (enabled) to quit?

I was once a participant in a televised panel discussion sponsored by the Roundtable of Christians and Jews. The general problem was racial conflict in the southern city where I lived; the specific topic was the practical aspects of integrating public schools. At one point in the debate, a panel member who had been silent for some time finally came forth with the ultimate pronouncement: "If we would all just obey the golden rule, there wouldn't be any problem." That bit of wisdom effectively killed the discussion for several moments. We all knew, of course, what we *ought* to do, our problem was finding some way we could afford to do it.

Even St. Paul, who was very fond of telling people what they ought to do, recognized the problem: "The good that I want to do is just what I cannot do." Nor is the dilemma exclusively a Christian one. The Roman poet Ovid observed, "I am not a man; I'm a civil war."

The preacher doesn't need to tell Christians to obey the golden rule or to love God and to love their neighbor. This philosophy predates Jesus Christ by many centuries and is not uniquely Christian by any means. Christians already believe strongly in this philosophy of life, and most would like nothing better than to live in a world where it was the norm of human attitude and behavior. Unfortunately, they don't; and, therefore, many cannot see how they can afford such a dangerous, expensive standard. If this is all there is to the Good News, then why Christ? Why a Christian religion at all? Surely Christ came for something more than to reiterate the religious teachings of Moses and the prophets. Or was he, after all, as the Muslims have been saying for hundreds of years, another in the succession of wise, articulate prophets? If so, "our Gospel is empty" and "we, of all men, are most greatly to be pitied."

Whereas the moral imprecations that emanate from the pulpit are of little or no value to the listener, they are at least easy to take—precisely because we already agree with them. On the other hand, when the preacher begins to share with us the news that could be of inestimable value, we may find the therapy more expensive than we had bargained for. The implications of living as one who is perfectly loved are terrifying. The burden of being forgiven may seem as intolerable as the burden of sin itself. We may not be able to bear it.

That is exactly the point. No one *is* able—he must be *enabled*. And that is the joy-filled task of the liturgical preacher: to show me how, and by whom, I am enabled to live as a forgiven one. No one, by himself, can afford it. But the price has already been paid! In one sense, to continue the metaphor, it is the down payment that has been prepaid; I have an obligation to continue the monthly notes, but even they have been securely underwritten. In other words, I really *can* afford it. Now, that's what I need to hear: what God has already done and is doing in loving and forgiving me. No one ever loved God or his neighbor because someone told him he ought to do so. Human love of God can only appear in response to God's prior love. When I have experienced such a love and have identified its source, then I am free to respond.

At the same time, the preacher must be wary of making light of my own role in the process. All of us have heard (or used) such phrases as: "All you have to do is accept God's love," or, "God's forgiveness is there, you merely have to accept it," or, "we only have to turn to God." All? Merely? Only? As though it were the simplest, easiest thing in the world. Anyone who has known the pain and struggle of turning to God, anyone who has experienced the humiliation of accepting such love and forgiveness, knows that the words "all," "merely," and "only" are simply inappropriate. Turning to God and accepting his love and forgiveness is not the answer—that is the problem!

The vocabulary of the preacher would be vastly improved by expunging from it the words "ought," "must," and "should," and similar terms and phrases when they are intended as moral imperatives. In addition, expressions such as "all," "merely," and "only" are unrealistic when they deprecate the expense and the pain involved in hearing and receiving the uncomfortable Gospel.

Fortunately, the liturgical preacher does not have to rely entirely, or even chiefly, upon his own words. There are the words and actions of the liturgy itself: the story, the autobiography of a community that knows itself as the body of Christ; the enactment of God's forgiveness and the community's acceptance; the great thanksgiving; the celebration; the community celebrating; the family table on which sacrifice is offered and received; the altar around which the family of God eats and drinks.

> Christ has died;
> Christ is risen;
> Christ will come again!

The very nature of the Sunday Eucharist is the celebration of the cosmic, eternal Christ event in the immediate situation of this fallen man. Fallen? Certainly. Guilty? You bet. But forgiven and healed and made worthy by God; resurrected into the new life in Christ—here and now. Now *that* calls for a celebration!

Chapter

10

CHAPTER AND VERSE

"JESUS loves me, this I know . . ." But it is not because "the Bible tells me so" that I know it. I know it because people tell me so—people whom I know love me and whom I can therefore trust. If they had just told me and then let it go at that, I still would not really *know* it. The true knowledge of God's love for me came, and still comes, through the experience of that love within a community that embodies his love. The Bible tells me *how*—that is, some of the ways in which God's love has been revealed to the world. The Bible tells us a lot of other things, too; but taken by itself, the Bible does not persuade anyone that God loves him today. Before anything can be "proved" by reference to the Bible, one must first be willing to accept the Scripture as authoritative. The Bible is not self-authenticating. Its authority for the individual lies in the community which claims it and proclaims it.

Through the years many books have been written about the necessity for a scriptural base for all theology. Volumes have also been forthcoming establishing biblical authority for the practice of preaching. We are still waiting for a good study on the authority exercised by the Bible on a majority of the people who claim membership in the body of Christ. I strongly suspect that it is minimal at best, at least among those in the principal traditions. Certainly it is true that one can no longer (if it were ever possible) make passing or subtle references to even the principal themes of the Bible and expect the average congregation to be able to identify any connection. Nor can one any longer (if one ever could) make explicit reference, even to quoting chapter and verse, and expect thereby to be persuasive. When the question "Sez who?" is raised, the response, "It says so in the Bible," may effectively silence the disrespectful inquirer, but one can hardly hope that it will carry much, if any, weight in determining belief, attitude, or behavior for most.

We are told that there was a time in the recent history of this country when Christians could be expected to have some familiarity with the content of the Bible, to have read it with some care, to have used it for devotional purposes, and to have given it at least some rudimentary study. Whether or not such an expectation was ever realistic, it seldom is the case today. As a publication, the Bible is unique: it continues to outsell every other book on the market (in some years, all other books combined), and yet it would be easier to gather a group of Christians conversant with the canon of Agatha Christie than one of like size whose members claimed equal familiarity with holy writ.

It simply is a fact that most Christians do not know the content of the Bible, are not familiar with its principal themes, and while continuing to honor and respect it in the abstract, do not acknowledge that it has ultimate authority over their lives.

This is a phenomenon which most preachers fully recognize, publicly lament, and mightily strive to reverse. Surprisingly, most preachers fail (or refuse) to grasp the single most obvious implication of the stubborn resistance of most Christians to make themselves familiar with Scripture: people are simply not that interested in it. They pay the Bible great respect, as they might the Queen of England; but, like the Queen, it has little or no authority over their daily lives. They expect the clergy to know the Bible, of course, and to tell them anything it contains

which might impinge directly upon them—much in the way
they expect their lawyers to be familiar with the legal codes,
and for many of the same reasons.

It is not my purpose to pass judgment on this phenomenon or
to offer any schemes or programs to correct it. I do want to call
attention to it and to explore some of the implications of this
state of affairs for the practice of preaching.

If the purpose of preaching is to bring the Good News to
people, to help them identify God working through Christ in
the world today, and if this news is apt to be unexpected, even
revolutionary, then it obviously is necessary to secure the fullest
kind of attention and participation on the part of the listeners.
The easiest way to do that is to begin where sensitivity begins—
with feelings that really matter to the life of the individual and
the congregation. One of the most difficult ways to effect full
participation, if not the single most difficult way, is to begin on
the cognitive level. Most Christians are interested in the Bible
to a degree, but the interest is chiefly academic and somewhat
similar to our interest in other significant historical documents.
No one denies its importance, but few are concerned with it at
the very core of their lives. On the other hand, all of us are
immediately responsive when touched in the areas of our pain
or pleasure.

The preacher who takes this seriously will begin where I, the
listener, really live—with that which I can immediately recognize as vital. Then I am willing to listen to anything he has to
say, because he is talking about how I can live. As listeners,
most of us are reluctant to begin the process of reasoning in the
hope that it will finally make some positive contribution to the
business of living. But if the preacher will *begin* with my life,
then I am ready, even eager, to reason.

This means that probably the best way to begin a sermon is
by avoiding the temptation to reread, restate, or paraphrase the
Scripture, or to launch into a lengthy (or even a brief) explanation of the historical setting or the meaning of the passage.

Many a good sermon—that is, one with helpful insights and a
creative proclamation of the Gospel—has been lost because the
preacher neglected to say at the beginning why it was important
for people to listen. Some of the difficulty here might possibly
arise from the normal structure of the liturgy itself. The usual
sequence followed by most liturgical formularies is that the
Bible reading is followed by the sermon. In fact, this order has
its own scriptural precedence in the story of Jesus' reading from
the scroll of Isaiah in the synagogue and then preaching on the
passage. Theoretically this is both the logical and dramatic
order. However, the effectiveness of this sequence presupposes
attentiveness to the reading itself as though it were really important, as though it really were news, and as though one were
eager to hear that news and to learn that it is good.

In your own experience, is this the attitude most people
bring to the liturgical event of hearing Scripture read? Unless it
is a familiar narrative such as one of the better known parables
or events in the life of one of the more famous figures, a majority of worshipers probably are unable to recall the Bible reading by the time the service is concluded. This is due to a combination of circumstances: people no longer expect *news* from the
Bible (after all, it's thousands of years old), they are unfamiliar
with the whole book and therefore have difficulty making sense
out of one brief pericope removed from its context; most importantly, it just *sounds* as though it would be boring.

It takes training, knowledge, skill, and lots of rehearsal to be
able to read aloud well. Most readers of Scripture in the liturgy
—including the clergy—have neither training nor inherent skill in
the technique of public reading; and almost none have put in
adequate rehearsal time. Liturgical reading of Scripture does
not require an ordained person, but to be effective it certainly
does require someone with training and talent in the art of
public reading. Simply being literate is no more a qualification
for such reading aloud than it is for singing a cantata.

And so, expecting little or nothing from the Bible reading
itself, few people really attend it, and none are "on the tip-toe

of expectation." Perhaps it would be more effective if the Bible reading were to follow the sermon rather than precede it. Then, the preacher could have pointed out what things to listen for and why. Then, it might have far more impact as a summary, an illustration, or a focusing of the sermon.

In any event, there is no need for the sermon itself to adhere to the sequence of the liturgy as a whole. Sermonic references to the Bible and quotations from it are most effective when they serve as a climax rather than as an introduction to any given point. And then they can be very effective indeed. Despite a lack of knowledge of the Bible, most Christians still feel that it should be normative for the Church, at least as an institution. They are pleased to learn that it confirms their experience—in fact, to many of them this comes as a pleasant surprise and can provide that ultimate goal of the communicator, an "Ah-ha!" experience. Furthermore, people are more apt to remember the reading when they can make such a connection. This is the source of authority.

All this places an even heavier burden of responsibility upon the preacher to be faithful to the message of the Gospel. What the congregation hears and comes to accept as truth depends in a large measure upon the preacher's integrity and lots of hard work. He cannot rely upon a reference or quotation to make his point for him. The Bible serves as corroboration of the sermon, not vice versa.

One of the advantages of this situation, as well as one of the dangers, is that it is possible to preach a thoroughly biblical sermon—that is, one that is strictly faithful to the message and that has sprung from study of the liturgical pericope—without ever making a single direct reference to or quotation from the Bible itself. Most preachers would not choose to do it this way very often because the Bible can, and usually does, provide a helpful dimension to the sermon which for many reasons enhances the proclamation; but the point is that it can be done this way and sometimes should be.

When I use the phrase "biblical preaching" and insist that

preaching be based upon and grow out of a study of the Bible as a whole and specifically the Scripture appointed for the day, I am not asking for specific references or quotations. In fact, many Christians, with justification, have become suspicious of such use of the Bible. They have heard holy writ quoted to prove opposite sides of the same question. Having little or no expertise themselves, they are forced to make their judgments on other factors and to disregard the claimed inherent authority of the Bible. They have learned from bitter experience that "even Satan quotes Scripture."

Over the years I must have heard several hundred sermons on the parable of the Pharisee and the publican praying in the Temple. Yet, I can count on the fingers of one hand those which did not include a discourse on pharisaic religion ("They weren't bad people—after all, they were the religious establishment of their time"), on the prayer habits of the Hebrews, on their practice of tithing, and so on. Is it surprising that the only ones I remember are those few sermons that spared me all the historical setting, clearly put God's redemptive act in my life, the life of the community at the center of the sermon, and then used the parable as an illustration?

There are, of course, times and contexts for serious study of the Bible where it is appropriate and helpful to explore the historical setting, to do form criticism and rigorous exegesis—and all of us, especially preachers, could stand a lot more of it—but not in the midst of a liturgical celebration. That is the time for the proclamation of the *results* of such study as they help to interpret and proclaim the Good News of the risen Lord.

In other words, it is important—essential—to say what Scripture is saying; it is not essential to identify the source, although it usually is helpful to do so. To "preach the Bible" means to be faithful to the biblical message. To be precise, it is not our task to preach the Bible, but to preach Christ—as he is revealed and interpreted in the Bible and as he continues to be revealed in the lives of men and women today and interpreted by the Christian community living as his body. God, working through Jesus Christ and revealed by the Holy Spirit, is the only proper subject for a Christian sermon. The Bible is the primary and indispensable source book for our preaching; it is not the subject.

The fact that people are genrally ignorant of the Bible requires more, not less, work on the part of the preacher in his efforts to be faithful to it. Thorough knowledge of the Bible is no longer (if it ever was) residual community property from which the preacher may draw. He has to do it himself, and this demands training, study, discipline, and many long hours; and there simply is no substitute for it. The further away from seminary they get, the less attention preachers seem to give to the essential business of exegesis and general Bible study. There are several factors that influence this tendency. In the first place, they already know so much more about Scripture than almost anyone else in their congregations that they can easily, and without being aware of it, come to assume that they already know most of what would be useful to them as pastors and preachers. Secondly, they, like the majority of Christians, have become disillusioned with the facile and prolific "proof text" use of biblical quotations. Also, for many the Bible has lost its urgency and vitality, and their interest is largely academic and pragmatic. And, of course, serious study of this kind takes time —lots of time—and most of us have so many demands on our limited time that we are loath to employ any significant amount of it in study. We have been taught to be "people-oriented" and have been led to believe that study is not a people-oriented activity.

But without this kind of study on a continuing and disciplined basis, the preacher soon becomes shallow and sometimes dries up altogether. After dealing year after year with the same lections for a particular Sunday, many preachers feel they have just about drained those pericopes of all their sustenance. On the other hand, I know preachers who preach several times each week on the same set of propers and who testify that it is only after the third or fourth year of wrestling with those texts that they finally break beneath the crust of the obvious and begin to tap the real life-giving core. Recently, many of the major Christian traditions have adopted a two-year or even a three-year cycle of liturgical readings. This has been advertised as being done for the benefit of the worshiper, in order that he be enabled to hear more Scripture over the course of three years. Actually, the one chance most people had of ever remembering the readings was by identifying certain of them with particular seasons of the year or activities of the congregation. Some years ago John Cheever could write in a novel:*

St. Paul meant blizzards. St. Mathias meant a thaw. For the marriage at Cana and the cleansing of the leper the oil furnace would still be running although the vents in the stained-glass windows were sometimes open to the raw spring air. Abstain from fornication. Possess your vessel in honor. Jesus departs from the coast of Tyre and Sidon as the skiing ends. For the crucifixion a bobsled stands stranded in a flowerbed, its painter coiled among the early violets. The trout streams open for the resurrection. The crimson cloths at Pentecost and the miracle of the tongues meant swimming. St. James and Revelations fell on the first warm days of summer when you could smell the climbing roses by the window and when an occasional stray bee would buzz into the house of God and buzz out again. Trinity carried one into summer, the dog days, and the drought, and the parable of the Samaritan was spoken as the season changed and the gentle sounds of the night garden turned as harsh as hardware. The flesh lusteth against the spirit to the smoke of leaf fires as did the raising of the dead. Then one was back again with St. Andrew and the snows of Advent.

In the future, with the adoption of the three-year cycle of readings, such identifications will be difficult at best, and the preacher will have an even greater responsibility. As usual, responsibility means work.

Many preachers have found it helpful to distinguish between

---

* From *Bullet Park,* by John Cheever. Copyright © 1969 by John Cheever. Reprinted by permission of Alfred A. Knopf, Inc.

homiletical exegesis—that is, exegesis done primarily for the preparation of a sermon—and the classical, more academic exegesis appropriate in the course of Bible study. In the first place, homiletical exegesis presupposes a thorough academic exegesis. Until the preacher has submitted to the discipline of a rigorous academic exegesis of the particular pericope, the homiletical work will be thin at best and soon will degenerate to the merely superficial. Important preaching cannot long survive on a starvation diet deprived of its primary source of protein.

Academic exegesis is tedious exacting work. However, it need not be repeated each time the preacher is faced with the same pericope—at least not in its entirety. Although biblical scholars are constantly discovering new material and developing new tools, much of the basic exegetical work (at least for most of us as nonspecialists) needs to be done only once, with a periodic review and updating of our findings. Homiletical exegesis, on the other hand, must be done each time. Whereas the more formal task is circumscribed by rules and strives toward precision, homiletical exegesis is much more freewheeling. It allows one to wander all over Scripture, making emotional as well as mental associations. This does not mean that the latter is undisciplined, although to the more formally trained it might appear to be so; it is simply that because the purpose is different, the methods are also appropriately different. The aim of homiletical exegesis is not technical precision but faithfulness to the Gospel message, richness of experience, and insights into the human condition. To do it well, the preacher must be familiar with the entire Bible, not just with favorite passages or books. Furthermore, this familiarity must be on several levels: content, theology, themes, literary style, and all those elements brought into play by the more formal academic study as well.

Homiletical exegesis, then, is not a way of avoiding the hard work of academic study; is is a way of cashing in on the results of that effort. It is more art than science. This means that it is so dependent upon the talents and resources of the individual

than imagining scholarly and academic queries. We all remember some cartoon similar to the one depicting a preacher leaning far over his gothic pulpit, shaking his finger at the two proverbial "little old ladies in the front row," and declaring: "Ah-ha! Now you'll be saying that is Sabellianism!" It is a natural result of our study, of course, but we preachers seem to have an uncanny knack of positing and responding to questions not a single person in our congregations would think of asking.

We can be rescued from this occupational hazard (and at the same time spare our bewildered listeners) by keeping uppermost the whole purpose of proclaiming the Good News of Jesus Christ: to bring and to celebrate the New Life.

Chapter

11

MAKING YOUR POINT

"Preachin' is like shootin' craps: if you don't make your point, it ain't nuthin'."

"THE REVEREND LEROY" *(Flip Wilson)*

SOME YEARS ago a famous preacher on the southern tent-meeting circuit was asked the secret of his power in the pulpit. The evangelist replied: "First, I read myself full; then, I think myself clean. I pray myself hot; and then—I LET GO!"

A good scheme. In addition to a highly developed skill, it also requires depth of study, hard thinking, and sweat-producing prayer. Most of us would like some sort of system or method for the weekly preparation of our sermons that is just a bit more explicit and at the same time fits our own particular work style and takes advantage of our own peculiar skills and resources.

Usually students and beginning preachers become aware of their need for some sort of system, at least as a starting point, when they begin to suspect that the time they spend on sermon preparation might be used more efficiently and creatively. Veteran preachers frequently discover that over a period of years they have gradually, and usually without realizing it, allowed the discipline of sermon preparation to slip away. Sometimes this has resulted in a nonsystem that leaves everything up for grabs each week, and what could and should be a joyous, stimulating part of their ministry has been reduced to a few frantic hours of laboriously fulfilling an obligation.

The value of beginning with a method, even if it is used chiefly as a point of reference and departure, is that ordering his time can free the preacher to tap his natural creativity and help him realize the fullest potential from the preaching event. Such a method—any method—should always be flexible enough to change and grow as the situation changes and the preacher grows. A few preachers resist the use of any method other than one they devise themselves. They correctly understand that finally each preacher has to discover his own individual work pattern, but they draw the conclusion that this means each preacher's method of sermon preparation is not debatable. As one said to me recently: "After all, thirty years of experience has got to count for something." Of course, it does. At the same time, anyone's method of doing anything—especially something as important as the proclamation of the Word—should always be open to challenge and change. It just could be that one had been making the same mistakes for thirty years; or, even more likely, that the method had not kept pace with the man. The best method of sermon preparation for any individual is one that has evolved over a period of years and has been continually tested and changed on the basis of experience and new learning. The change is the result of growth, not of deterioration.

What follows is a method of sermon preparation that has been developed by and for me. It is always in the process of evolution, and as I set it down it is not a final product, nor will it ever be. The various components are not original; the scheme is highly eclectic and I do not hesitate to adopt any useful idea. Once an idea has proved helpful, and I have incorporated it into my own way of working, it becomes mine, no matter what may have been the original source. The only claim made for this particular scheme is that it has been useful to me, and in one form or another, to many others. Use all or any parts of it. Rearrange, modify, and adapt as suits your individual needs and purposes. If none of it seems particularly helpful to you, try another, preferably one that has been tested over a period of time by someone you trust. Any system will require individual adaptation. The goal is to discover what is the most helpful for you in your present situation. I do not adhere to this scheme invariably, and I feel not the slightest twinge of conscience on those occasions when I approach the task of sermon preparation in an entirely different way. It does provide a helpful base to return to whenever I seem to be going so far astray that I am in danger of being lost. It is offered here with the hope that it may be as helpful to you.

First, the bare outline of seven steps in sermon preparation; then some explanatory notes on each.

Preparing the Sermon

STEPS TO BE TAKEN—TIMES AND TIMING

HOURS*

1. READ THE PROPERS *1) Saturday (immediately after preparation of next day's sermon)* 1/2
   2) Sunday evening (repeat in another version) 1/2
   a. All Scripture appointed for the liturgy, including psalms, graduals, preface, etc.
   b. Read in at least two versions.
2. SELECT and EXEGETE TEXT *Monday—without fail* 2
   a. Do it yourself first.
   b. Turn to commentaries and other aids afterwards.
3. DETERMINE PROPOSITION: BUILD PROSPECTUS
   Monday or Tuesday 1
   a. Proposition: 1) What is the problem, need, or situation with which the sermon is concerned?

*A note about the amount of time. The times are intended to indicate the relative amount of time spent on each step, not necessarily the actual time. Some sermons take longer to prepare; some come together much more quickly. Times are shown chiefly to keep the several steps in proportion.

       2) What Good News does the sermon proclaim in response?

       3) What response to that Good News is urged?

  b. Write out the proposition as a single statement, if possible.

  c. Prospectus:
      1) Proposition statement.
      2) Tentative conclusion and introduction.
      3) Tentative ideas for outline development.
      4) Notes of illustrations and special points.

4. PERIPHERAL READING AND NOTING *Tuesday thru Friday*
  a. As you read, make calls, etc., bring sermon to mind.
  b. Bathroom or yard work tryouts.

5. FIRST DRAFT, OR OUTLINE, OR RECORDING *Friday*   3 to 4
  a. Use all possible material.
  b. Don't be too concerned with order.
  c. Make constant reference to theme statement (proposition).
  d. Fix opening, closing, any special points and illustrations.
  e. Make a tentative arrangement of order.

6. FINAL PRODUCT *Saturday (or Friday)*   3 to 4
  a. Arrange in final order.
  b. Review and sharpen language.
  c. Check for needless repetitions.
  d. Prepare manuscript for reading aloud: style punctuation.
    Or—Final outline: Include all necessary proper names, dates, statistics, quotations.
  e. Arrange materials for easy handling in pulpit.

7. REHEARSAL *Saturday*
  a. In the study: standing up; record and playback.
  b. In the pulpit.

8. READ PROPERS FOR NEXT WEEK *(see #1 above)*

---

11 to 13

Step 1:   Usually one is at the height of enthusiasm for preaching when the preparation and rehearsal of a sermon is just concluded. This is the time, then, while one is still caught up in the excitement of the enterprise, to read through the proper lections appointed for the *following* Sunday. Just read them through, that's all. At this stage, don't try to formulate even the germ of a sermon for the next week; your whole attention is and should be focused on tomorrow. A simple read-through, however, will cause one to make all sorts of surprising connections later. Then, on Sunday afternoon or evening, read them through again in another version. Besides fixing the lections in the preacher's mind for the purpose of preaching, this has the added advantage of familiarizing him with the Scripture before beginning detailed plans for the liturgy itself. Thus, liturgy and sermon begin to take shape at the same time and the possibilities for exploiting the inherent interdependence are more apparent.

Step 2:   Again, the advantages of doing the exegesis early in the week are both homiletical and liturgical. Steps 3 and 4 below depend upon having done the exegesis.

Step 3:   The three questions in what I call the proposition were first developed, so I am told, by Professor Henry B. Adams of the San Francisco Theological Seminary as an aid for listening to sermons. I have adapted them for the preacher to use as a primary step to sermon preparation.

1) What is the problem, need, or situation with which the sermon is concerned?
2) What Good News does the sermon proclaim in response?
3) What response to that Good News is urged?

This may be the most crucial step in the scheme; it certainly has proven to be the most useful to preachers who have incorporated this idea into their own methods. Experience has shown that most sermon inadequacies can be traced to failure to deal with and respond to these questions at the very beginning. It will be seen that they bring into focus much of what has been discussed in the preceding chapters.

Each question should be answered in a single, simple sentence. Do not set forth theological generalities here; be quite specific. It is helpful if the response to the first is phrased as a question, the second phrased as a positive statement, and the last as an invitation. These responses are not intended to become a part of the sermon itself. Rather, they tell the preacher what he intends to be doing in this particular sermon and serve as a test of each step along the way and of the final product. The three responses might lend themselves to a single statement, which then becomes a thematic statement. This is not always possible and certainly is not essential; but it is helpful because it's easier to work with a single statement than with three.

The key here is to be sure that the problem, need, or situation is one out of real life rather than out of the preacher's study. "Why did Jesus say that the publican was justified rather than the Pharisee?" is not a real-life question. Not a single person in the congregation is really concerned about that at all. On the other hand, "How can I live with the fact that I am a sinner?" or "What does God expect of me?" are questions that might trouble any Christian.

In responding to the second question, include an estimate of the cost—the implications of receiving the Good News and allowing it to become normative for one's life. The third question is asking just what sort of reaction/response the preacher would like to see as a result of the sermon. The response might be physical, intellectual, emotional, or a combination of these. If we know clearly what sort of response we would like, we will have some indication whether or not our sermon has done its work.

Whether in a single sentence or in the form of question, statement, and invitation, the responses should be written out.

In either form, they provide the theme for the sermon and the first, and essential, element in what I have called a prospectus for the sermon. The second item in the prospectus is a tentative concluding paragraph and a tentative opening paragraph. Note that the final paragraph is written first. This is so that the preacher will know where he is heading and will know when he has arrived. However, these two paragraphs should be prepared with the full understanding that they are strictly tentative and are subject to change as the sermon develops. One may change the point of destination as the road unfolds, but unless one has some definite destination in mind before starting out, the result is apt to appear to be aimless wandering.

Part of the prospectus, which is begun early in the week, is some preliminary (and again, tentative) notes on the development of the sermon itself. One idea for the mechanics of this is to write out the propositional or thematic statement(s) at the top of a sheet of paper. Then draw a line, and underneath enter whatever thoughts occur for the development of the sermon. The tentative opening and concluding paragraphs might be written on the back for easy reference. This sheet of paper can be left on the preacher's desk or carried in a pocket so that as other ideas occur through the week they can be added to the preliminary notes.

Step 4:   If one has done the three steps outlined above, then the sermon (and the liturgy itself) will be brought to mind constantly as the preacher goes about the daily routine of reading, making calls, attending meetings, watching TV, and so on. He can scarcely avoid making connections between the sermon idea and life as it is being lived in his community. Here is where the very "stuff" of preaching comes from. There can be no question of relevancy—life and the Gospel are seen as a single piece. One may find oneself formulating ideas while shaving or taking a shower or doing yard work. I have preached my best sermons to a towel bar in my bathroom. The advantage of such bathroom or backyard tryouts is the opportunity to verbalize one's ideas, to say them out loud and see if one can really put them into coherent sentences.

Step 5:   Now is the time to get all possible material down in the form of notes or rough draft or tape recording. At this stage, use everything that has occurred to you through the week, without too much concern for order. Then you will be in a position to prepare a final version of your opening and closing paragraphs. One caution: make constant reference to the thematic or propositional statement to be sure that each of the components of the sermon contributes to your purpose. Here you may discover that you have some very good ideas that you would like to use but that somehow just don't fit this situation. Be ruthless with yourself. If it makes you feel better, file the irrelevant material away for future use; don't try to include everything you happen to think of in a single sermon. Remember what one parishioner said of the preacher: "He tried to tell everything he knew in twenty minutes—and he succeeded."

Here, too, is the place to give careful consideration to how the liturgy can contribute to the proclamation of the Word, complementing and supplementing the sermon. We are so word-oriented that we frequently forget that liturgical action is a powerful communicating agent. How does this sermon get reflected in the liturgy? What can we leave unsaid in the sermon because it is better said in the liturgy?

All this raises the question of the length of the finished product. How long should a sermon be? Before the twentieth century it was not uncommon for a preacher to hold forth for as much as two hours, and if the sermon were much shorter than an hour, parishoners were apt to complain that the preacher was shirking his duty. The trend today is toward much shorter sermons, usually fifteen to twenty minutes, although thirty-minute sermons are common in many places. Certainly one of the contributing factors to the gradual but definite decrease in preaching time has been the influence of television. In a television drama the average shot by a single camera is less than thirty seconds. Even the full-front picture of the newscaster seldom holds for over a minute, and we are accustomed to receiving our entertainment and information in ten- to twelve-minute segments at the longest. One result of this has been a conditioned shortening of attention span.

The advantage to a longer sermon (say thirty minutes or more) is that it gives the preacher an opportunity to dig beneath the surface of an issue, to probe a question at depth, and to utilize a variety of resources. The problem is that most of us are unaccustomed to speaking this long at a stretch and we run the danger of needless repetition, of bringing in extraneous and irrelevant material, and of becoming just plain boring. The shorter sermon has the advantage of making a single point, or just a few, with sharpness and clarity. It runs the risk of superficiality, but sheer length is no guarantee against that danger.

It seems to me that the length of time should be determined by the sermon and not the other way around. If, on any given morning, the preacher can say clearly what he has to say in five minutes, there is no compelling reason why he should preach any longer. On the other hand, if the particular communication takes twenty minutes to share, then he should take the twenty minutes without apology. If the preacher is bringing the Good News of life itself, time itself is not the governing factor. Five minutes or twenty-five, when the subject is my resurrected life I want to hear what Good News there is for me today. The sensitive preacher will take this responsibility seriously; that is, he will use all the time necessary to effect the communication and will not squander it by using more than is helpful in the given situation.

STEP 6:　This is a continuation of the previous step and might even be done at the same time period. The several components of the sermon having been tested against the propositional statement, now is the time to see that the remaining material is arranged in some coherent order. Remember that the listener doesn't have a copy of the script, so he can't refer back. Nor can he stop the whole process while he catches up or makes a connection that escaped him. So, it is important that the interconnections or transitions be clear and that the whole thing move along in a logical sequence. One way to test this is to see if one's sermon can be outlined according to the old classical formula one learned in intermediate-school English class. The formal outline structure should look something like this:

INTRODUCTION: *May or may not be an integral part of the outline.*
I. BASIC POINT: *One or several; normally not over three.*
    A. PRINCIPAL SUBDIVISION
        1. DEVELOPMENT OF SUBDIVISION
            a. ILLUSTRATIONS: STORIES, ALLUSIONS, QUOTATIONS
CONCLUSION: *May or may not be an integral part of the outline*

A good outline reads logically from the smallest divisions to the largest. That is, all the lower-case material should contribute directly to the Arabic numeral immediately preceding; all the Arabic numeral material should lead up to the capital letters; and all the capitals should lead up to the Roman numeral. Such an outline is for the purpose of ordering the sermon only and is not intended for use in the pulpit as an actual preaching outline. If the sermon will not outline in this fashion, one surely should question the arrangement. Perhaps some element is in the wrong place. Perhaps one or more elements simply do not fit into this sermon in spite of the fact that they seem to be relevant to the theme. Also, by using the test of outlining, one can readily spot needless repetition as well as lacunae in the presentation. Furthermore, it should clearly show whether one is devoting too much time to matters of relatively small importance and too little to areas the preacher feels are paramount.

The outline for preaching—that is, the one to be used in the pulpit—is strictly a visual mnemonic device for the benefit of the preacher. It does not need to follow any rules. Its only purpose is to remind the preacher of what to say and when. Thus, it may be in phrases, complete sentences, or single words, or any combination of these. It may employ Roman numerals, letters, and so forth, or it may be just a series of notes, one following the other and all with apparently equal value. It should contain everything that helps the preacher remember what he wants to say, but it need not contain anything more than what he actually needs. His old English teacher will never see it, so it can be strictly a utilitarian document. No matter what it looks like, if it serves the purpose of reminding the preacher at the proper time, it is a successful outline.

A seemingly endless and totally irrelevant debate rages over the relative merits of preaching from a full manuscript, an outline, a few notes on an index card, or with no notes at all. The answer, of course, is that the most successful method is the one that succeeds. There are advantages and disadvantages to each; but the point of preaching is proclamation through verbal communication, and the best method is the one that enhances that purpose.

Use of a full manuscript has the advantage of freeing the preacher from concern about how best to verbalize his ideas. He can be more relaxed and can concentrate on his delivery. He doesn't have to be worrying about the sermon throughout whatever portion of the liturgy precedes it; nor does he have to be concerned later about whether he said it well. He can take the pains to polish his language and be confident that the sermon represents the very best articulation he knows how to give the particular ideas. On the other hand, effective manuscript reading is a skill possessed only by a very few, usually highly trained, people. Generally, it is not taught in seminaries. Unskilled reading can render a masterful manuscript ineffective. The late vice-president of the United States, Alben Barkley, used to tell the story of his first political speech. When he asked his grandfather what he thought of it, the old man replied that he had only three criticisms: "In the first place, you read it. In the second place, you read it poorly. And in the third place, it wasn't worth reading in the first place." Assuming that the sermon is worth reading in the first place, it deserves to be read well.

Each of the other methods has similar advantages and disadvantages. Every preacher, however, could become more effective by training himself to use all of the several methods. Of course, each individual will find himself usually more comfortable with one than with the others; but he won't know which is actually best for him unless he really tries them all. Furthermore, some situations and some sermons just seem to call for one style above others, and the preacher should be professionally competent enough to be able to choose the style most appropriate for the sermon and the situation.

Step 7: Rehearsal is probably the most frequently neglected step in sermon preparation, especially by experienced preachers. The reason, of course, is that over the years they have developed a certain self-confidence in their ability to deliver the sermon once it has been adequately planned or written; and by omitting a rehearsal, they will save an hour or so of precious time. Also, there seems to be some embarrassment suffered by many preachers in the act of preaching to an empty house. But consider the fact that the most accomplished musician—one who, at least on tour, will perform the same works several times a week—would not think of appearing without a rehearsal. Even the average church choir would not attempt a familiar anthem without a rehearsal. And these people are doing something they've done before. The preacher may protest that his sermon is no more important than the choir's anthem or the organist's solo, but surely he will admit that it is at least *as* important. It can be demonstrated quite easily that almost anyone in the congregation can tell with unerring accuracy whether or not the preacher has rehearsed the sermon. They may or may not appreciate it when it has been rehearsed, but they can almost always tell when it has not.

Clarence Rivers once said of the liturgy that "spontaneity requires careful rehearsal." The same is true for the sermon, whether it is preached from a manuscript or delivered extemporaneously; spontaneity is not diminished by rehearsal when the preacher is talking about the most important, vital, and compelling thing in his life.

And so, after the rehearsal we arrive at the final step, reading next week's propers, the first step in the preparation of next week's sermon.

Before we leave the subject of sermon preparation, it is important to consider the use of language and vocabulary. Someone has said that "habitual verbalization in terms of polysyllabic terminology is infinitely to be preferred. The utilization of this eventuates in a felicitous obfuscation of the material to which reference is putatively established, minimizing the probability of comprehension and, consequently, of congregational discombobulation." But don't you believe it!

People have at least two vocabularies: one for writing and reading and another for speaking and listening. Our reading vocabulary is vastly larger than our listening one. Words that we easily recognize and understand in print may be meaningless to us when we hear them spoken—not so much because we don't know their definitions, but because being unused to speaking them ourselves and hearing them spoken, we really do not hear the word properly. Furthermore, in the process of reading, we have time to dissect the word, to think about its possible meanings, to relate it to its context, and so on. This leisure is not afforded us when we are listening to the spoken word. Take the word "redemption," an example we used earlier

(p. 22). It is a perfectly good theological word, and you and I know what it means. So, in fact, do many people if they see it written and have time to think about it. But carrying its theological definition it is scarcely a common word in our listening or speaking vocabulary. Almost invariably when we use the word redemption, or hear it used, it has something to do with S & H Green Stamps. It can be a communicating word in a sermon, of course; but it should be used carefully and with full consideration of how it will be understood by the listeners. It may be that another phrase entirely would carry the particular concept more successfully.

The purpose of the sentence is not merely to make sense—it must also carry the message. In the spoken medium this usually means that simple, direct statements are more effective than complex ones, and that conversational words are to be preferred over words that might be perfectly appropriate in a written piece. This is not to suggest that the preacher "talk down" to a congregation. Nor does it mean limiting himself to the so-called basic English vocabulary or resorting to crude language of the streets. It is to say that the preacher must constantly be listening to himself as he writes. If possible, speak the sentences—and the whole sermon—into a tape recorder. When listening back, try to listen as one who has never heard it before and who hasn't given much thought to the subject. As religious professionals, we have developed a kind of shorthand language that is of great benefit when communicating with other professionals but that may block communication with those outside the profession—that is, with almost everyone to whom we preach. This tendency is not unique to clergy; most professions develop their own shorthand, and most of it is difficult at best for the layman. Have you ever tried to read the show business magazine *Variety?* Imagine how much sense it would make if you heard it read aloud. Sit in with a group of doctors or sailors or printers who are "talking shop." As long as they are speaking to one another, their shorthand actually enhances their communication. As laymen in those fields, we are reduced to nodding sagely and hoping we have at least caught the general drift of what they're saying.

Some wag once compiled a "Theological Thesaurus" to demonstrate the way many of our favorite theological phrases have lost their vitality. With only slight modification, it could easily be adopted by preachers.

Homiletical Thesaurus

For those who would be more relevant in their preaching vocabulary, the following is offered as a foolproof device. Keep this chart handy on your desk or posted on a bulletin board over your typewriter. Whenever you are at a loss for a relevant phrase in your sermon, or whenever you would enhance communication by using more meaningful language, simply cast a pair of dice for three rolls. At each roll, note the word indicated by the corresponding number on the chart. Three rolls will automatically produce a phrase which may be used in any situation or sermon.

TOTAL ON DICE	1ST ROLL	2ND ROLL	3RD ROLL
2	Personal	Human	Celebration
3	Total	Eucharistic	Being
4	Integrated	In terms of	Crisis
5	Authentic	Grass roots	Witness
6	Real	Transitional	Response
7	Optional	Chardinian	Commitment
8	Incarnational	Christian	Identity
9	Communal	Existential	Encounter
10	Fulfilling	Experimental	Relationship
11	Relevant	Ecumenical	Love
12	Rich and meaningful	Implemental	Dialogue

CAUTION: Be sure to construct your phrase in the order indicated by the column headings; reversal or rearrangement of the order will result in unauthentic communication!

In the spoken medium, the best word is not always the most precise; the best combination of words is not always the most brilliant. One who knew this quite well and was a master practitioner was the late Winston Churchill. He wrote out all his speeches. Yet, he resisted the temptation to say: "Dispatches from the zone of hostilities indicate that the military situation on the continent has deteriorated to an alarming extent." Instead, he said simply, "The news from France is very bad." And no one ever questioned Sir Winston's erudition.

Sermon preparation can be one of the most stimulating and rewarding experiences of the preacher's week, second always to the preaching event itself. It calls for a method or system that the particular preacher feels comfortable with, and a discipline that is flexible enough to allow for the exigency of the time while being tight enough to free him from decisions about what to do next so that he can concentrate on the needs of the people and the Word acting to meet those needs.

Chapter

12

A SPECIALIZED FORM
OF LITURGICAL PREACHING

NOT too many years ago some churchgoers would admit that one of the chief reasons they preferred to attend an early morning celebration of the Eucharist on Sunday was to avoid having to listen to a sermon. Both clergy and lay people (although for entirely different reasons) would merely have laughed at any suggestion of a sermon at a regular weekday celebration.

When the situation changed, it did so suddenly and dramatically. Now, many clergy would no more think of omitting the sermon from the liturgy than they would of leaving out the epiclesis—and their parishioners would be more likely to be aware of the omission of the former than of the latter. Almost overnight (or so it seemed) thousands of priests began the long-neglected practice of expounding the Word at *every* celebration —even if, as in most cases, it was only a two- to three-minute exposition of the Gospel pericope just read.

Technically, this form of the sermon is known as a postil (rhymes with Gospel). The dictionary defines a postil as a short sermon on a Scripture passage, "especially on the Gospel or Epistle for the day."

The postil is a unique sermonic form. In the first place, it is brief—and today, by our practice, we are defining brief as no more than five minutes. In the second place, it is based directly and obviously upon the Gospel pericope read that day (or the Epistle, or both). Thirdly, it is informal in style, both as to language and delivery.

These restrictions mean that the postil simply cannot be merely a shortened version of the more full-blown fifteen- or twenty-minute sermon. The whole shape and style is different; the intent is different; and the preparation likewise must be different.

For instance, there is just no time in a postil for an introduction, nor for a conclusion in the sense of wrapping up the major points of the sermon in a summary. In fact, there is no time for more than a single point. The preacher must get to that point quickly, state it clearly and succinctly, and then quit. There is no time to restate the pericope in modern language. (If that is important, it should be read in a modern version to begin with.) The preacher has just read it aloud. The sequence is that he reads the passage, closes the book, and expounds it—with no intervening ceremonies. The postil, then, may take the form of drawing the congregations's attention to a single idea or point being made by the Scripture. In that case, there probably will be no time for an illustration—the pericope provides the illustration. On the other hand, the postil itself may take the form of an illustration—just that, with no further explanation, provided the illustration actually does illustrate. Or, again, the postil may seek to raise to consciousness one important implication of accepting the truth of the Good News.

The postil is always delivered in a liturgical setting, and therefore might be considered as a paradigm for the liturgical sermon. It can easily highlight the theme of the celebration, which is then picked up by the prayers of intercession or in the preface, and reinforced by hymns and psalms. It probably should always lead directly to a liturgical response such as prayer or offertory, and inevitably to Communion itself. The point is that the postil, even more than the regular liturgical sermon, doesn't have to go it alone. It must rely on other elements of the liturgy to illustrate and expand. The single point cannot be belabored; it can only, and needs only, to be stated clearly. Perhaps the postil will take the form of a question raised, of a challenge posed, or of an invitation extended. In any case, the preacher must resist the temptation to provide all the answers or to wrap things up in a neat package for his listeners. It should be what McLuhan would call a "cool" medium, in which the listener must participate if there is to be any message at all, and to which he must contribute if that message is to make any difference.

In form, the postil is always kerygmatic. It definitely does not have moral exhortation as its chief intent, although it may well imply some form of ethical behavior. Likewise the postil does not primarily seek to educate, at least not in the didactic or catechetical sense—although not infrequently it does raise to the level of consciousness some realization that at best had been held only tacitly. And certainly the postil is not exegetical in form, in spite of the fact that its preparation requires thorough exegesis.

Stylistically, the postil is usually less formal than the regular sermon and therefore probably best presented extemporaneously. However, extemporaneous does not mean impromptu. On the contrary, an effective postil requires the most careful preparation and rehearsal. Although the number of hours required to prepare a postil is probably fewer than for preparing a full sermon, the proportion of preparation time to delivery time is far higher. Again it was the "Veep," Alben Barkley, who said that if he were invited to speak someplace for ten minutes, he liked to have a month's notice; if the speech was to last for half an hour, he should have two weeks to prepare; but if he were to be allowed an hour—well, he was ready any time.

In an electronic age, the postil may very well be the most effective way of proclaiming the Good News orally in a liturgical setting. It is a relatively new form of preaching for most of us, and we still have a lot to learn about its potential and its use. The use is already so widespread, and the potential apparently so promising, that it has earned the right to special and serious attention as a unique form of gospelling with its own integrity. Already we know that it requires a different sort of cooperation on the part of the congregation. They may not be accustomed to listening as intensely as the postil demands. They may have to learn a new style of listening, to receive supplemental input from stimuli other than the preacher's words, both before and after the sermon proper, and to provide their own contribution to the communication.

Lately, there has been some experimentation with a slight variation. Actually, the postil itself remains the same in style and intent, but the format changes somewhat to incorporate two postils in the same service. The order is: First Reading (Old Testament or Epistle) followed immediately by a postil; then, perhaps, a gradual hymn or psalm. The Gospel reading is followed immediately by a second postil. In this situation, one must be careful that the postils are really sermons rather than commentaries. When the lections have been carefully chosen, this format can very effectively employ two preachers, each making the same point but on the basis of two different portions of Scripture.

In those parishes where the postil has been given an appropriate amount of thought, study, and careful preparation, both clergy and congregations are enthusiastic about it. It is an encouraging sign that the sermon will survive the electronic age and continue to be a vital means for proclaiming the Good News of the Christ event for today.

Chapter

13

ON HAVING THE LAST WORD

WHETHER he uses it well or poorly, every preacher spends time in the preparation and delivery of his sermons. Whether he is faithful to it or not, virtually every preacher finds the source of the Word he proclaims in the Scripture and tradition of the Church. But there is another primary resource for preaching—namely, the congregation itself. Preachers tend to be rather possessive about their sermons—that is, no matter how much they may like or despise the weekly task, it is an obligation they feel they must and should bear alone. Preaching is thought of as a solitary thing—something one person does for the benefit of others. As a result, preachers do not normally look upon their congregations as a resource for the preparation of a sermon; their role is to listen.

Most congregations and most members of congregations assume the same thing. Occasionally, they might offer words of encouragement or of criticism (the latter, usually to their friends rather than to the preacher), but they really don't expect to be consulted about the preaching. After all, that's what they hire a preacher for. That's his responsibility and, in the eyes of many, about the only thing he does.

In the last decade or so, more and more preachers have come to realize that they could be taking advantage of this rich resource. While acknowledging that the ultimate responsibility for each sermon must lie with the preacher alone, they are beginning to see the task of sermon preparation as one that can be shared profitably with members of the congregation. Furthermore, given the theological position developed in the first part of this book, it is not only helpful to involve the congregation in the preaching enterprise, it is essential to do so. This same statement has a different kind of force when put in reverse order: not only is it a theological necessity for the worshiping community to be a part of the whole process of preaching, it is helpful to both preacher and congregation.

The second form of that statement is important because many preachers, while acknowledging the validity of the theory of community participation, fear that in practice it would be more of a barrier than an aid to creative, prophetic preaching. They fear that the congregation would effectively limit the subject matter of sermons, making some subjects and even some ideas taboo. They are concerned that the preacher would lose his individuality and become a sort of hack writer grinding out sermons based on scenarios provided by others and, since truth cannot be arrived at by group process, such sermons would become like the proverbial horse assembled by a committee, emerging as a camel. In addition, most preachers are convinced that they know their congregations very well indeed, that they know their levels of understanding, their areas of knowledge and ignorance, what makes them feel comfortable and what is disturbing to them, and their needs, felt and unrealized. The difficulty is that few preachers have any reliable means of testing their presuppositions or discovering the truth about how the congregation sees itself.

Most of the objections to involving the community in the process of sermon preparation are based on a single bad experience or, much more likely, on no experience at all. No book is going to succeed in overcoming all the various objections that might be leveled at a proposal for community responsibility for preaching, especially if those objections grow out of a fear, conscious or unconscious, on the part of the preacher. However, for those who are willing to acknowledge at least a grain of truth in the theological position I have been taking, and who are anxious to utilize any resource that might be creative, I can offer some suggestions. These are based upon the contributions of a good many people, upon the experiences of a number of practicing preachers in a variety of situations, and upon my own experience with several entirely different types of worshiping communities.

Sermon feedback or reaction groups have been used for many years in one form or another. The term "feedback" indicates that the function of the congregation or the group is to react. From such feedback, the sensitive preacher will discover ways of improving his oral communication in the future. More important than helping the preacher refine his skills, reaction sessions provide an opportunity for the members to think about the points made in the sermon and how they pertain to their own lives and to the life of the community. It encourages them to contribute their own ideas and suggestions by providing a "safe" place where this can be done without embarrassment or fear of being put down. Here, in community, they can ask questions for clarification, take issue with something the preacher said, supplement his insights, or begin to push the thought even further and in entirely different directions. However, we want more than just reaction to a given sermon—we want *pro*-action: involvement at the beginning of the process as well as at the end. Such preinvolvement will drastically alter the character of the subsequent reaction and will tend to make it even more responsible.

One way to obtain this kind of involvement in the ongoing process of preaching week in, week out is to form a group with a rotating membership of eight people. Two new people are added to the group each week and each person agrees to serve for four weeks and then to drop out, thus maintaining the number eight. This is not difficult to do in almost any parish; most people will agree to serve if they know in advance that they will be expected to commit themselves for only four weeks. Of course, it would be possible to run the same program with twelve people on a four-week cycle (adding and dropping three each week) or with ten on a five-week schedule, but experience and experimentation has shown that the eight-person, four-week plan is easier to maintain and, on the whole, provides the maximum benefit for both preacher and participants. Members of the group may be designated by any method of random selection and either by the preacher himself or by some other member of the congregation who agrees to assume that responsibility.

Participants are asked to commit themselves for one hour each Sunday for the four weeks of their tenure. Ideally, this time should be scheduled immediately following the period of worship, although in rare circumstances it might be desirable or even necessary to schedule it for some time later in the day or evening. It should not, however, be postponed beyond Sunday evening. In the first place, we know that the retention level drops drastically over a twenty-four-hour period. More importantly, any delay beyond Sunday would seriously diminish the contribution of the group for reasons that soon will become apparent.

Probably the best place for the group to meet is in the preacher's study or office, if it is large enough to accommodate that many people. At any rate, it should be someplace that affords privacy and an atmosphere that is both businesslike and yet conducive to relaxation and freedom. The session is divided into two distinct parts, each lasting exactly one-half hour.

Although it may seem backwards, the function of the group will be more easily understood if I describe the latter half-hour first. The second thirty-minute period is devoted to "feed-forward," or *pro*-action, aimed toward the sermon for the following Sunday. Every member of the group has been informed in advance of the proper lections appointed for the next Sunday and has been asked to read them over prior to the meeting. The preliminary reading and subsequent discussion may encompass all the lessons provided (Old Testament, Epistle, and Gospel) or may be restricted to one or two. In either case, this should be determined by the preacher in advance and communicated to the several members. Participants should be encouraged to make notes, mental or manual, of any questions raised by the reading, whether these be questions of fact or of meaning and significance. Now, with the preacher present as a resource, the group proceeds to discuss the appointed Scripture. This is not intended to be a Bible study period, although naturally there will be some similarity. The purpose of the discussion is to ask questions about the meaning of the readings to the individuals present and the significance, if any, of those portions of Scripture for those people living in that particular community during that particular week.

As the discussion progresses, the role of the preacher is chiefly one of listener and resource person. He is not there to suggest answers, although he might briefly clarify some question of fact if it seems to be impeding the discussion. He may, depending upon the level of participation by the members of the group, suggest questions himself or suggest areas in which questions might be raised. Meanwhile, the preacher should be making notes about the discussion. It must be made very clear to all that while the preacher may use any or all of this material in the pulpit next Sunday, he is not obligated to do so. If circumstances seem to dictate, he may take an entirely different approach with the sermon. He makes no promises one way or the other.

But note the dynamics of the situation. As the preacher does his own exegesis of the Scripture the next day, and as he begins to build a prospectus early in the week, he will already know what eight people in the congregation think about those passages. Also, he knows that at least eight people will be present the following Sunday who have read the Scripture in advance and have given it some thought. He knows, too, that there will be eight people really listening to his sermon. Finally, he knows that six of those listeners, plus two new ones, are going to have an opportunity to react to what he says and that they surely will do that in light of the previous discussion. All this is virtually certain to influence his preparation. It is not intended to dictate or govern the direction his sermon will take, but it should provide him with a rich resource of material from which to draw.

Following the sermon, the six continuing group members meet with their two additional members and begin the first half-hour of their session. It is at this point that the feedback or reaction to this week's sermon occurs. Generally, there are two different foci for such feedback discussions. One is the subject matter itself (*what* was said), and the other is the style or form of its presentation (*how* it was said). The latter is helpful only when it enables the preacher to see how his manner of presentation enhanced the gospelling or in what ways it restricted the proclamation or inhibited the hearing of it. This is dangerous ground because reactions to style are usually based on matters of individual taste, and these vary so greatly, change so frequently, and depend upon so many variables, that it is extremely difficult to assess the value of any particular comment or set of comments. Unless the preacher, or some other person who can serve as group leader, has had special training and experience in handling this sort of taste/value-judgment session, it probably would be wise to avoid deliberately eliciting response to the *how*. This is most easily done by consciously focusing upon the *what*. If reactions to style or manner are really significant, they will be mentioned anyway and, in that case, should be carefully noted by the preacher.

To be most effective, a reaction session should not be too long —a relative matter that is determined chiefly by the number in the group. If there are eight people, half an hour should be sufficient time to allow everyone to make their most important contributions to the discussion and to stimulate thinking so that conversation can later be extended beyond the immediate group. If people know in advance that they have a limited time, and are informed precisely as to what that limit is, they will tend to be responsible in the use of it. With some practice they can become very efficient and can provide an enormous amount of material in a very brief time span.

For this period it is best that the preacher is not present, but that he provide a small tape recorder with exactly thirty minutes of tape. He might come in and begin the recorder for the group, or he could ask someone else to do that for him. At any rate, the members of the group would know that when the tape ran out, they were through. Also, they should be advised that the preacher will listen to a playback of the tape sometime during the coming week—probably on Monday. It should go without saying that the preacher must take this as a solemn responsibility and attend carefully to the tape every week without fail. Not only does he have this obligation to the participants of the group, and thereby to the community, but the whole purpose is to provide him with help—and surely we all need all of that we can get.

There are several reasons for the preacher's absence during this period. First of all, he is apt to be occupied elsewhere; the first thirty minutes following the worship are usually a busy and important segment of the clergyman's week for a lot of reasons. Also, some people feel more at ease saying honestly what they think about the sermon if they don't have to look the preacher in the eye while saying it; and this is true whether their comments are favorable or unfavorable. At the same time, they are apt to be more responsible if they know their remarks are being recorded and will be listened to by the preacher. Finally, if the preacher isn't there, he won't be tempted to retort—either to defend his position or to explain or clarify something. After all, what the people heard is what they heard. If eight of them heard something the preacher did not intend, or if some of them heard one thing and some heard another, then the preacher may assume that that is fairly representative of the way the congregation as a whole heard it, and he'll just have to live with that. It's too late now to clarify, explain, or defend.

With only thirty minutes at their disposal, it is important that the group have some structure and direction for their discussion. Here is where we use Professor Adams's three questions more in the manner in which he intended them; but note the subquestions inserted to bring the discussion down to specifics:

1. What was the problem, or need, or situation with which this sermon was concerned?
   Is this a life question, a real need, a realistic situation?
2. What Good News did the sermon proclaim in response to #1?
   Was the news appropriate? Was it really good? Did it help?
3. What response did the sermon elicit from me?
   How will the sermon actually affect me, if at all?

These questions might be printed on a poster or piece of newsprint attached to a wall where everyone can see, or they might be mimeographed and copies distributed to everyone. In either event, all participants should understand that they are to address their remarks to these considerations. Different groups will utilize this structure in different ways. Some will adhere to it strictly, some may ignore it entirely, but most will deal with the various parts of it to the degree they think them important. If they can respond helpfully to only one of the three questions, in terms of the added subquestion, the preacher will learn a great deal that should not only enrich his insights into the community but also aid him in the preparation of subsequent sermons and in the development of his communication skills.

When the tape runs out, the feedback segment comes to a close. Now, the preacher joins the group and the emphasis shifts to feed-forward. And so it goes, week in, week out. The preacher is in constant touch with those who listen to his sermons, and they are in communication with him. Real dialogical preaching can take place, in a literal sense.

The benefit of such a reaction/proaction plan is not restricted to the preacher. As he begins to gain insights into the community, members of the group do also. They have an opportunity to get in touch with some of the thoughts and feelings of their fellow worshipers that they may never have been sensitive to before, and on matters that really count. And, of course, they come to know the preacher even as he comes to know them, to understand some of the problems he wrestles with each week, and to appreciate the level of commitment he has to the business of gospelling in their midst. Within a relatively short period of time a fairly healthy percentage of the congregation will have been trained to listen, perhaps on a level they had not known before. They might acquire the habit, and even discover the joy, of listening.

Soon, the problem will not be one of recruiting for the group but of explaining to people why they must drop out after only four weeks and why they cannot be asked to serve more frequently. One moderate size parish I know now has three such groups going all the time. Naturally, the preacher can attend only one feed-forward session, but the others work with a tape recorder for both segments of their meeting, and the preacher listens to all of them. In another parish, former group members continue to meet for both reaction and proaction simply for their own benefit. Both these preachers have expressed their astonishment, and their chagrin, at how hungry the people were.

Any plan to involve the worshiping community in the total process of sermon planning costs a little time and effort and requires a lot of openness and humility. Those who are eager to attempt anything to enhance the gospelling in their communities, and those who simply are desperate enough, may find the very things they most need—courage, support, and confidence —to be the chief benefits accruing from sharing this part of the Lord's ministry with other members of his body. The Word belongs to the worshiping community which embraces both congregation and preacher.

A PERSONAL POSTSCRIPT

I HAVE a great personal investment in the preaching enterprise. In the first place, I earn my living by doing it and by trying to help others discover how they can do it. Also, I believe firmly the theological necessity of proclaiming the Good News, in season and out, through the spoken words of men and women. I am thoroughly convinced that within the context of the liturgy the preached Word can have the power of God's grace—to heal, to absolve, to unify, to reconcile, to raise to new life. Actually, I am more interested in the salvation of people than I am in the salvation of preaching; but I believe that faithful gospelling can play a significant role in that process. Also, I just like to preach and to hear good preaching.

I believe that the preacher is not so much called as he is sanctioned. Preaching is more a privilege than an obligation—a privilege carrying with it a grave responsibility that deserves to be taken seriously and exercised diligently.

Bonhoeffer once said that "preaching is the riches and the poverty of the Church." By "poverty," Bonhoeffer meant that the Word of God suffered the humiliation of being revealed through the words of human beings. By "riches," he was expressing his belief that the Word was the most valuable possession the world could have and the one thing essential to the existence of the Church. Inscribed on many pulpits and lecterns is the quotation from the Fourth Gospel: "We would see Jesus." It is finally and supremely in the liturgical action which includes Word and sacrament that the preacher can respond to that request with joy and confidence: *"Ecce homo!"*

NOTES

Chapter 1

Anthony Trollope, *Barchester Towers* (New York: Oxford Univ. Press, 1953).

H. H. Farmer, *The Servant Of The Word* (Philadelphia: Fortress Press, 1942).

Alexander Schmemann, *The World As Sacrament* (London: Darton, Longman and Todd, 1966).

Edward-H. Schillebeeckx, "Word and Sacrament and the Church" in *Listening* (Winter, 1969).

Chapter 2

Among the many studies on communication theory which provide the basis for these propositions, the following are useful surveys of the field:

W. B. Bennis (ed.) *et al, The Planning Of Change* (New York: Rinehart and Winston, 1962).

Frank E. X. Dance, *Human Communication Theory* (New York: Rinehart and Winston, 1967).

Chapter 3

Schillebeeckx, *Op. Cit.*

Georges Gusdorf, *Speaking* (Evanston, Ill.: Northwestern University Press, 1965).

Chapter 4

D. W. Cleverley Ford, *Preaching Today* (London: Society for Promoting Christian Knowledge, 1969).

William D. Thompson, *A Listener's Guide To Preaching* (Nashville: Abingdon Press, 1966).

William Temple, *Nature, Man and God* (New York: Macmillan and Co., 1949).

Chapter 6

George M. Bass, *The Renewal Of Liturgical Preaching* (Minneapolis: Augsburg Publishing House, 1967).

Reginald H. Fuller, *What Is Liturgical Preaching?* (London: Student Christian Movement Press, 1957).

Domenico Grasso, *Proclaiming God's Message* (Notre Dame, In.: University of Notre Dame Press, 1965).

Karl Barth, *The Preaching of the Gospel* (Richmond, Va.: John Knox Press, 1962).

J.-J. von Allmen, *Preaching and Congregation* (Philadelphia: Westminster Press, 1963).

Schillebeeckx, *op. cit.*

Chapter 8

Dale E. Bussis, *Princeton Seminary Bulletin* (March, 1964).

Donald F. Chatfield, unpublished notes mimeographed for classes in preaching.

Chapter 10

Richard Leucke, *Violent Sleep* (Philadelphia: Fortress Press, 1969).

Chapter 11

Clarence Rivers, *Celebration* (New York: Herder and Herder, 1969).

Some portions of Chapter 13 originally appeared in my article "It Rhymes With Gospel" in *The Anglican: Vol. 5, No. 22* (Summer, 1975) and are used here by permission.